FLAGSHIP HISTORYMAKERS

FDR

KATHRYN COOPER

 erCollins*Publishers*

Dedication

For my mum and dad.

Published by HarperCollins*Publishers* Ltd
77–85 Fulham Palace Road
London
W6 8JB

Browse the complete Collins catalogue at
www.collinseducation.com

© HarperCollins*Publishers* Ltd 2004
First published 2004

ISBN 000 717324 5

British Library Cataloguing in Publication Data. A
catalogue record for this book is available from the
British Library.

Series commissioned by Graham Bradbury
Project management by Will Chuter
Edited by Hayley Willer
Book and cover design by Derek Lee
Map artwork by Richard Morris
Picture research by Celia Dearing
Index by Julie Rimington
Production by Sarah Robinson
Printed and bound by Printing Express, Ltd.,
Hong Kong

ACKNOWLEDGEMENTS

The Publishers would like to thank the following
for permission to reproduce pictures on these pages
(T=Top, B=Bottom, L=Left, R=Right):

© Corbis 7, 9, 10, 25R, 26, 42, 51T,
© Bettmann/Corbis 14, 19, 25L, 57, © Oscar
White/Corbis 12; *Oh, so that's the kind of sailor he
is*, cartoon by J.N.'Ding' Darling, 1937 © J.N.'Ding'
Darling Foundation 51B; Getty Images/New York
Times Co./Archive Photos 36.

Cover picture: portrait of Franklin D Roosevelt
© Corbis

Every effort has been made to contact the holders
of copyright material, but if any have been
inadvertently overlooked the Publishers will be
pleased to make the necessary arrangements at the
first opportunity.

You might also like to visit
www.harpercollins.co.uk
The book lovers' website

Contents

Why do historians differ?

THE purpose of the Flagship Historymakers series is to explore the main debates surrounding a number of key individuals in British, European and American History.

Each book begins with a chronology of the significant events in the life of the particular individual, and an outline of the person's career. The book then examines in greater detail three of the most important and controversial issues in the life of the individual – issues that continue to attract differing views from historians, and that feature prominently in examination syllabuses in A-level History and beyond.

Each of these issue sections provides students with an overview of the main arguments put forward by historians. By posing key questions, these sections aim to help students to think through the areas of debate and to form their own judgements on the evidence. It is important, therefore, for students to understand why historians differ in their views on past events and, in particular, on the role of individuals in past events.

The study of history is an ongoing debate about events in the past. Although factual evidence is the essential ingredient of history, it is the *interpretation* of factual evidence that forms the basis for historical debate. The study of how and why historians differ in their various interpretations is termed 'historiography'.

Historical debate can occur for a wide variety of reasons.

Insufficient evidence

In some cases there is insufficient evidence to provide a definitive conclusion. In attempting to 'fill the gaps' where factual evidence is unavailable, historians use their professional judgement to make 'informed comments' about the past.

New evidence

As new evidence comes to light, an historian today may have more information on which to base judgements than historians in the past. For instance, major sources of information about 20th-century United States history are the presidential libraries of past presidents. The FDR presidential library in Hyde Park, New York State, contains a large number of FDR's public papers. Only when this information becomes available, can historians develop a more objective view of the past. This was the case with Robert Dallek's *Franklin D. Roosevelt and American Foreign Policy 1932–1945* (1995).

A 'philosophy' of history?

Many historians have a specific view of history that will affect the way they make their historical judgements. For instance, Marxist historians – who take their view from the writings of Karl Marx, the founder of modern socialism – believe that society has always been made up of competing economic and social classes. They also place considerable importance on economic reasons behind human decision-making. Therefore, a Marxist historian looking at an historical issue may take a completely different viewpoint to a non-Marxist historian. This is the case with Howard Zinn's *A People's History of the United States* (1980). Zinn is a 'new left' historian.

The role of the individual

Some historians have seen past history as being largely moulded by the acts of specific individuals. Presidents, such as Abraham Lincoln during the US Civil War or Franklin D. Rooesvelt, can be picked out as having helped change US history. Other historians have tended to play down the role of individuals; instead, they high-light the importance of more general social, economic and political change. Rather than seeing Harry Hopkins as a leading New Deal reformer, these historians tend to see him as a representative of the social reform wing of the Democratic Party of the New Deal years.

Placing different emphasis on the same historical evidence

Even if historians do not possess different philosophies of history or place different emphasis on the role of the individual, it is still possible for them to disagree in one very important way. This is that they may place different emphases on aspects of the same factual evidence. As a result, History should be seen as a subject that encourages debate about the past, based on historical evidence.

Historians will always differ

Historical debate is, in its nature, continuous. What today may be an accepted view about a past event may well change in the future, as the debate continues.

Timeline: FDR's life

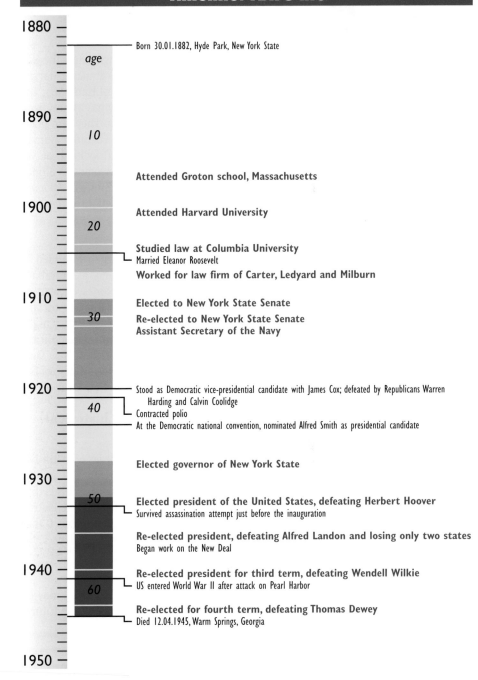

1880

Born 30.01.1882, Hyde Park, New York State

age

1890

10

Attended Groton school, Massachusetts

1900

Attended Harvard University

20

Studied law at Columbia University
Married Eleanor Roosevelt
Worked for law firm of Carter, Ledyard and Milburn

1910

Elected to New York State Senate

30

Re-elected to New York State Senate
Assistant Secretary of the Navy

1920

Stood as Democratic vice-presidential candidate with James Cox; defeated by Republicans Warren
    Harding and Calvin Coolidge

40

Contracted polio

At the Democratic national convention, nominated Alfred Smith as presidential candidate

Elected governor of New York State

1930

50

Elected president of the United States, defeating Herbert Hoover
Survived assassination attempt just before the inauguration

Re-elected president, defeating Alfred Landon and losing only two states
Began work on the New Deal

1940

Re-elected president for third term, defeating Wendell Wilkie

60

US entered World War II after attack on Pearl Harbor

Re-elected for fourth term, defeating Thomas Dewey
Died 12.04.1945, Warm Springs, Georgia

1950

Franklin Delano Roosevelt in his first presidency (1933–6).

FDR: a brief biography

How did FDR make history?

Four terms: until FDR, US presidents often stood for election twice, serving two four-year terms, but by tradition they did not stand more than twice. In 1951, the twenty-second amendment was added to the Constitution limiting all future presidents to a maximum of two terms.

Federal Government: the national government.

The only president to be elected for **four terms**, Franklin Delano Roosevelt is perhaps the most important president of the 20th century. He came into office at a time of crisis, when the Great Depression threatened the American economic and political system. He entered the White House promising a 'New Deal' for the American people and, with his administration, he embarked on the biggest programme of social legislation the country had ever seen. Through his cheerful optimism and his mastery of the media, he gained massive public support and made the American people believe in their country again. He used the power of the **Federal Government** to tackle the economic crisis and to try to put people back to work and save them from degrading poverty. He also went beyond the immediate problem and, through programmes such as the introduction of social security, he ensured that the American people would not suffer such a catastrophe again.

Instead of retiring after his second term, FDR broke with tradition and stood again to lead his country when he saw it threatened by the growth of totalitarianism across the world. He led a reluctant public into a more active foreign policy, supporting the British in their stand against the Nazis. When the attack on Pearl Harbor brought America directly into the conflict, FDR was able once more to use the power of the Federal Government to organise the nation's resources for victory.

Throughout his life, FDR believed in the power of government to do good for people and the power of the US to be a force for good in the world. He worked to achieve these ends in both domestic and foreign policy. In doing so, he expanded the power of government at home and abroad. Franklin Delano Roosevelt changed the perception and the reality of the American Government. In many ways, it could be claimed that he created the modern presidency.

Upbringing, education and marriage

Franklin Delano Roosevelt was born on 30 January 1882, only son of James Roosevelt and Sara Delano Roosevelt. It was James's second marriage, and he was 25 years older than Sara. Franklin's mother was domineering and overprotective, and for most of his childhood Franklin's father was ill. It was a lonely upbringing but the young Roosevelt learned to remain friendly and outwardly cheerful. He had

Upstate New York: New York State is one of the states of the USA. The state capital is Albany, although the largest city is New York. New York City is on the East coast, so inland parts of the state are often referred to as 'upstate'.

what might be termed an 'aristocratic' upbringing. Life in Hyde Park in **upstate New York** resembled that of the British upper classes, with country pursuits and a closed circle of powerful acquaintances.

When he was 14, Roosevelt was sent to Groton Boarding School in Massachusetts. He was an average scholar but he got on well with his teachers. Groton, under the headship of Reverend Endicott Peabody, was a massive influence on Roosevelt's development. The school had strong Christian values and the boys were encouraged to take part in 'good works'. Roosevelt was taught that privilege carried with it a duty to help those less fortunate. It is not difficult to see how this theme of responsibility for others was central to the whole philosophy of the New Deal.

In 1900, Roosevelt left Groton and went to Harvard University where he studied History and Government. At Harvard, his grades were mediocre but he earned a reputation as a good debater and, from 1903, he edited the college newspaper. After graduating from Harvard, Roosevelt attended law school at Columbia University until 1907.

While at Harvard, Roosevelt started dating Eleanor Roosevelt (his fifth cousin once removed), and they married in March 1905. Eleanor was an intelligent and serious young woman, and the favourite niece of Franklin's hero, **Theodore Roosevelt**. The couple had six children within 10 years, one of whom died at only 7½ months old. It was a happy marriage with mutual affection and respect until 1918 when Eleanor discovered her husband had been having an affair with his social secretary, Lucy Mercer. Eleanor gave Franklin an ultimatum to end the affair or the marriage. He did not see Lucy for over 20 years, but during his final days he met her again and she was with him when he died.

After the affair, Franklin's and Eleanor's marriage lost its intimacy and became more of a business partnership. Eleanor found the social entertaining, required of a president's wife, tedious. However, her own interests in issues, such as women's rights, poverty and racial discrimination, led her to develop her own political career.

Theodore Roosevelt (1858–1919)
Born in New York City into a wealthy family, Theodore Roosevelt worked as a civil service commissioner and later as a police commissioner. He was Assistant Secretary of the Navy from 1897 to 1898 but resigned to fight in the Spanish-American War. In 1898, he became governor of New York State and then vice president to William McKinley. When McKinley was assassinated in 1901 Roosevelt, at 42 years old, became the youngest president in America's history. He greatly expanded America's role in the world and, in 1906, he won the Nobel Peace Prize for mediating the end of the Russo-Japanese War.

Woodrow Wilson (1856–1924)
The son of a Presbyterian minister, Wilson became a professor of History and Political Science. He became governor of New Jersey in 1910 and then, in 1912, he was elected Democratic president, winning only 42 per cent of the popular vote but an overwhelming electoral vote. He won election again in 1916, largely because he kept the US out of the war that was raging in Europe. However, Wilson supported the Allied cause and, in 1917, the United States entered World War I, with the President promising to 'make the world safe for democracy'. After the war, Wilson tried to ensure peace through the creation of the League of Nations, but the American people did not want to get entangled in European affairs and the Senate refused to ratify the Versailles Treaty.

She wrote a column in a daily newspaper, worked with pressure groups to develop legislation, and represented her husband on many occasions at home and abroad. Eleanor was a great political asset to Roosevelt. She increased support for the President and his policies among the disadvantaged, especially among African-Americans with whom she did a massive amount of work.

Entering the political world

After passing the New York State bar examination at law school, Roosevelt worked as a lawyer. However, he did not enjoy the work and soon followed his real ambition to enter politics. In 1910, aged 28, he ran for New York State senator and became the first Democrat in 32 years to win in the twenty-sixth district. He was soon noticed in Washington, especially due to his support for **Woodrow Wilson** in the 1912 election campaign, and, in 1913, he was offered the position of Assistant Secretary of the Navy. Roosevelt relished this post as it had previously been held by Theodore Roosevelt. As Assistant Secretary, he was arrogant and made no secret of the fact that he believed he would go far. However, he also developed a reputation as hard working and efficient. When Europe exploded into war in 1914, the American public felt that it was not their concern. Roosevelt, on the other hand, believed that the US should militarily prepare itself in case it were called upon to fight. When the US did enter the war, in 1917, Roosevelt was instrumental in increasing naval production and instituting a programme of officer training.

By 1920, Roosevelt was sufficiently well known to be offered the nomination of vice-presidential candidate for James Cox. Unsurprisingly, the Democrats lost the election as they were split over many issues, notably drink, race and tariff reform. Although they lost, Roosevelt campaigned vigorously and made 1000 speeches in 32 states. He gained invaluable experience and national exposure so that he would be ready for his own assault on the White House in the next election.

Return to private life

In the meantime, Roosevelt returned to his private life and formed his own law practice in New York City.

In the summer of 1921, he became very ill and was diagnosed with **polio**. He refused to believe that he would not walk again, and both he and his wife were determined not to give up on his political ambitions. He went to Warm Springs, Georgia, to recuperate at a

Polio: (poliomyelitis) an infection of the nerves in the spinal cord that causes paralysis.

Understanding FDR

- **A man from a wealthy and privileged background**, who, nevertheless, had the 'common touch' and was loved by the poor and the disadvantaged who saw him as their friend.

- **A man of tremendous energy**, who was active and sporty, who loved sailing, but who was severely limited by his disability.

- **A man of great determination** but also a man who would delay making difficult decisions.

- **A man of great personal charm**, who enjoyed life and work.

- **A man who understood the importance of the media**, who was brilliant in his handling of journalists.

- **A man who loved being president**, who saw the White House as his rightful home.

- **A man of faith in God**, who firmly believed in the power of the American Government to do good and improve the lives of American citizens.

- **A man who had firm belief in democracy and capitalism**, both in America and as values for the world.

- **A man who believed that the United States should take an active role in international affairs**, who believed that the policy of isolationism did not always serve American interests.

> *'He was the President of the forgotten man and of all men.'*
> *Chicago Sun*, April 1945

run-down institution for polio sufferers. Over the years, he spent more than $200 000 developing the institution into one of the leading centres in the United States for the study and treatment of polio. In spite of the support and treatment Roosevelt received, he was never able to truly walk unaided again. This was a fact hidden from the public throughout his life by careful stage management. Despite this, Roosevelt's experiences in Georgia opened his eyes to some very important issues. He met many other people with disabilities who did not have his financial resources to help ease their lives. He also met people, many of them black, who could talk to him about their poverty and despair at a time when America was entering the biggest economic boom in its history. Many historians agree that Roosevelt's illness and disability gave him **empathy** for the disadvantaged, which someone of his background rarely had.

Empathy: an understanding and awareness of the feelings of others.

Governor of New York State

In 1928, Roosevelt was elected governor of New York State but, within a year of him taking the position, the Depression hit. **Herbert Hoover's** Republican Government was slow to act, believing that the economy would straighten itself out if it were left alone. Hoover had in fact attempted to reform banking even before the Wall Street crash but Congress rejected his proposals. When the Depression did come, Hoover eventually put forward several measures for relief and public works but again many were defeated by a hostile Congress. Roosevelt was much quicker to see the scale of hardship that the Depression was causing and was much quicker to act. In 1931, he introduced the Temporary Emergency Relief Administration to pay for public works for the one million unemployed in New York State. There were also schemes to provide food, clothing and shelter. Roosevelt's response to the crisis contrasted sharply with the seeming inaction of the Republican Government. It was hardly surprising, given what he achieved in New York State, that Roosevelt stood for, and won, the presidency in 1932.

The presidency

In 1933, Franklin D. Roosevelt (FDR) became the thirty-second president of the United States and was faced with the worst domestic crisis since the US Civil War of 1861–5. The stock market had crashed; banks, businesses and farms had gone bankrupt; millions of people had lost their savings and almost a quarter of the workforce was unemployed. Despite this, FDR did what he had done

Herbert Clark Hoover (1874–1964)

Born in Iowa, Hoover trained as a mining engineer. As chairman of the American Relief Committee, working to prevent famine in Europe after World War I, he gained a reputation as an effective administrator. From 1920 to 1928, he was Republican Secretary of Commerce for Harding and Coolidge and, in 1928, he was elected president. Within seven months of taking office, the Wall Street crash hit. Hoover believed that the economy would get better by itself, so he gained a reputation for having done nothing to tackle the Depression. After his defeat in 1932, Hoover returned to private business. In 1946, he again worked to relieve hunger in Europe. He headed the Hoover Commissions (1947–9, 1953–5), which investigated, and made recommendations on, the organisation of the Executive Branch of the US Government.

Prevailing economic orthodoxy: the view held by most people at the time regarding the economy; in this case the view that economies have natural cycles of boom and bust and one should not interfere in this.

Struck down: declared them unconstitutional so that they could no longer be applied.

Oil embargo: the banning of the sale or export of oil.

Isolationism: the policy of keeping out of the affairs of other states. Isolationism was followed by successive Republican presidents during the 1920s and early 1930s.

Lend-lease: a Bill, passed in March 1941, gave the President the power to lend-lease; to sell, transfer or exchange war materials to any nation whose defence he believed was vital to the USA.

'Four freedoms': freedom of speech, freedom of religion, freedom from want, freedom from fear.

in New York State; he put to one side the **prevailing economic orthodoxy** and experimented. During the election, he had promised a 'New Deal' for the American people, and over the following six years his administration introduced a massive programme of measures to deal with the economic crisis. In the first '100 days', alone, Congress passed 15 major Bills. There were also important reforms, including the first measure of social security in US history. FDR took ideas from his own experience in New York State, from the out-going Republicans and from his own group of advisers, nicknamed 'the Brains Trust'. His personal energy and enthusiasm, however, did as much as any New Deal policy to make people believe in their country again. His 'fireside chats' on the radio were not only a landmark in political use of the media, but they were vital in improving American morale during the Depression.

The support of the public for FDR was made clear when he took 46 out of 48 states in the 1936 presidential election. However, the scale of the victory made him over-confident. The Supreme Court had **struck down** several New Deal measures, such as the Agricultural Adjustment Act in 1936, and looked to be ready to do the same to some of FDR's reforms, such as the Social Security Act of 1935. So, in 1937, FDR proposed to reform the Supreme Court. He wished to introduce compulsory retirement for judges over 70 years old, and also wished to add six new judges. This 'Court packing plan' worried friends and enemies alike. The latter accused him of acting like a dictator, and the President was forced to withdraw his Court Reform Bill. FDR then made his situation worse by trying to influence the result of the 1938 congressional elections so that his critics would not be voted in. This intervention backfired and criticism of the President increased. If 1936 was the highest point of the FDR administration, 1937/8 was its lowest. However, foreign affairs soon began to take attention away from the problems of the Supreme Court.

Just as FDR took office in the USA, Hitler became chancellor of Germany. Tensions in Europe led to the outbreak of war between Britain and Germany in 1939. Not only that, but relations between the United States and Japan had been getting worse throughout the decade, with the US imposing an **oil embargo** on Japan in July 1940. FDR was torn between America's policy of **isolationism** and the view that America could best prevent war and protect itself by supporting Britain. Neutrality Acts prevented FDR from giving much active support but he gave material help to the British through **lend-lease** in 1941. He also met with Churchill on a ship off the coast of Newfoundland in August 1941, where he talked about the **'four freedoms'** necessary to create a secure world. In spite of the failure of the League of Nations, FDR still believed some kind of democratic international organisation could help make the world a better and safer place. The discussions laid the foundations of the future United Nations organisation.

On 7 December 1941, the Japanese attacked the American bases at Pearl Harbor in Hawaii. FDR's speech to Congress the following day spoke of 'a day that will live in infamy'. The US was now at war with Japan and, when Hitler declared war on America five days later, FDR was able to make common cause with the Allies.

Throughout World War II, FDR worked well with Churchill and **Stalin**. They met periodically to discuss strategic issues and the post-war world, for example at Teheran, Yalta and Potsdam. Some historians and contemporaries accused FDR of being too soft with the Russians, thus leaving some of the problems that Truman had to deal with during the Cold War. However, FDR helped maintain good relations with two very difficult men, while making decisions that affected the lives of millions. He might not always have been candid with his Allies but FDR was an astute politician and he knew the necessity of compromise, such as that made over Poland. Like others in the administration, FDR had hoped for freely elected governments in Eastern Europe but all that he could get from Stalin regarding Poland was a promise that non-communists would be part of the provisional government that the Soviets intended to set up. Politicians in the West had little hope that this promise would be fulfilled, but the reality, as FDR knew, was that the Red Army occupied the East. To force any policy on Stalin would mean conflict. Besides, at Yalta FDR believed he needed Stalin to help defeat the Japanese. A promise was all that he could realistically achieve.

FDR, however, did not live to see the end of the war. His deteriorating health was already giving his doctors concern during the 1944 election. Early in 1945, he took a break to recuperate and was in Warm Springs having his portrait painted when he complained of a headache. On 12 April 1945 Franklin Delano Roosevelt died, aged 63. Mourners lining the tracks wept openly as the train carried him back to his Hyde Park estate for burial.

Stalin (Josef Vissarionovich Dzugashvili) (1879–1953)
Stalin was a revolutionary from the Russian province of Georgia. He worked closely with Lenin during the Russian Revolution and was Communist Party General Secretary in the new state. He became Soviet leader in 1929. He implemented modernisation policies in agriculture and industry but was also responsible for millions of deaths during the purges.

1

New Deal: success or failure?

> **Did the New Deal bring about economic recovery?**

> **Did the New Deal 'save' America?**

> **How radical was the New Deal in protecting working people?**

Framework of events

1932	Nov	FDR elected thirty-second president of United States
1933	Mar	'100 days' begins with Emergency Banking Act
		Civilian Conservation Corps (CCC)
	May	Federal Emergency Relief Administration (FERA)
		Agricultural Adjustment Act (AAA)
		Tennessee Valley Authority (TVA)
	Jun	National Industrial Recovery Act (NIRA) establishes National Recovery Administration (NRA), including what becomes Public Works Administration (PWA)
	Nov	Civil Works Administration (CWA)
1934	Jun	Securities and Exchange Commission (SEC)
1935	Jan	Second New Deal begins
	Apr	Works Progress Administration (WPA)
	May	Supreme Court declares Title I of the NIRA unconstitutional (PWA unaffected)
		Rural Electrification Administration (REA)
	Jul	National Labor Relations Act
	Aug	Social Security Act
1936	Jan	Supreme Court declares AAA unconstitutional
	Feb	Soil Conservation and Domestic Allotment Act
	Nov	FDR elected for second term
1937	Jun	FDR cuts government spending and unemployment starts to rise
1938	Apr	Increase in spending to off-set 'Roosevelt recession'
	Jun	Fair Labor Standards Act
1939	Sep	Outbreak of World War II in Europe
1940	Nov	FDR elected for third term
1941	Dec	US enters World War II after attack on Pearl Harbor
1944	Nov	FDR elected for fourth term
1945	Apr	FDR dies in Warm Springs, Georgia

W HEN Franklin D. Roosevelt took office in March 1933, the United States was facing its worst crisis since the US Civil War of 1861–5. The new president promised a 'New Deal' for the American people. Consequently, expectations for the administration were high. FDR did not disappoint them. The next eight years saw America transformed, with programmes for the financial system, schemes for the unemployed, measures to help industry and agriculture, as well as policies that took the USA in a whole new direction, such as the introduction of social security. The impact of the New Deal was immense; every American government since has consciously tried to build on it or tried to dismantle it.

In the 1950s and 1960s, US presidents, Democrat and Republican alike, attempted to build on the legacy of the New Deal to a greater or lesser extent. Historians of the period such as William E. Leuchtenburg (*Franklin D. Roosevelt and the New Deal, 1932–1940*, (1963)) saw the New Deal as a success, albeit a qualified one (see **Landmark Study** below). FDR had managed to balance the needs of business and employees, of farmers and industrialists and saved America from the kind of extremism that the Depression gave rise to in Europe. Despite this, the problems faced by the United States in the 1960s and 1970s over civil rights, poverty and Vietnam led many historians and writers to look more critically at American **capitalism** and how it operated. These 'new left' writers are much more critical of FDR and the New Deal. They argue that capitalism had brought about the crisis of 1929 and the American Government should have taken the opportunity to change the economic and political system in a much more radical way. They argue that FDR was far too cautious and gave in too much to the interests of big business and the big banks. Historians such as Paul K. Conkin, in *The New Deal* (1968), and Howard Zinn, in *New Deal Thought* (1966), see the New Deal as a wasted opportunity.

Capitalism: an economic system that is based on the private ownership of property and individual wealth.

Landmark Study   **The book that changed people's views**

William E. Leuchtenburg, *Franklin D. Roosevelt and the New Deal, 1932–1940*
(Harper & Row, 1963)

This chronological study, which emphasises the role of FDR himself in shaping the New Deal, is still considered by many to be the best single text on the New Deal. Leuchtenburg is a liberal writer who recognises the shortcomings of the New Deal but, nevertheless, believes that it laid the basis for economic recovery and brought about some fundamental changes in American social policy. He sees the New Deal as a flawed but revolutionary period, where FDR laid the foundation for economic recovery and worked to help the weak in society who had previously been ignored. This book, for a long time, has been the 'standard' liberal view of FDR and the New Deal and, although it has been challenged from both the right and the left, it is probably still the most widely held interpretation.

Historiography: the differing views and explanations that historians have of events in the past.

Monetarist: economic view that argues for a free market with minimal government interference; control of the money supply and interest rates should be used to direct the economy, not government spending.

Keynesian: named after British economist John Maynard Keynes, who argued that governments should get out of depression and reduce unemployment by spending, even if it means going into debt.

To an extent, the **historiography** of the New Deal has followed the economic trends of the periods in which the historians were writing. In the 1980s, with the growth of right-wing politics and **monetarist** economics, historians began to criticise the **Keynesian** nature of the New Deal. Historians like Milton Friedman, in *Free to Choose: A Personal Statement* (1980), argue that far from doing too little, the New Deal had done too much and stifled recovery by too much interference from the Federal Government. They also point out that this growth in federal power did not end with the New Deal but remained and set a trend that has seen the Federal Government continue to grow and continue to expand its power into more and more areas of life.

In the last two decades, historians have once again given FDR and the New Deal a better press. By looking beyond the White House, historians like Anthony J. Badger, in *The New Deal: The Depression Years, 1933–1940* (1989), have pointed out the constraints under which FDR operated. No American president can do just as he likes, and taking into account the pressure from Congress and the restrictions of the Supreme Court, not to mention the conflicting needs and desires of the various groups within American society, the New Deal in fact achieved a lot.

Did the New Deal bring about economic recovery?

FDR's reaction to a financial crisis

When FDR took office, the American financial system was in crisis; businesses were losing money, farmers were losing their land and families were losing their homes. Above all, 25 per cent of the workforce (almost 14 million people) was unemployed. The New Deal attempted to tackle all of these problems and much more. Any visitor to the US can see the physical evidence of the New Deal, which produced 3700 playgrounds, 1050 airfields, 500 water treatment plants, 19 700 miles of water pipes, 822 000 miles of roads and streets, 122 000 bridges, 8000 parks, 22 000 housing projects, electrification for 780 000 farms and much, much more. But did the New Deal bring recovery to the economy?

Anti-trust legislation: anti-trust laws prohibited companies from joining together to fix prices. The laws were put in place to ensure competition among businesses.

Did FDR achieve industrial recovery?

To stop the wasteful competition that was driving down prices and profits, FDR introduced the National Industrial Recovery Act of 1933 (NIRA), which suspended **anti-trust legislation** and set up the

National Recovery Administration (NRA), which got groups of companies together to set 'codes of fair competition' – prices and production levels – for their particular industry. The Act also set a minimum wage and maximum working hours, and abolished child labour. It has been estimated that the NIRA created two million jobs and increased purchasing power by $3 billion. However, few people would disagree with Anthony J. Badger's comment, in *The New Deal: The Depression Years, 1933–1940* (1989), that 'the success of New Deal efforts to secure industrial recovery was strictly limited' and, in spite of its stated aim, the New Deal did not solve the problem of overproduction. The traditional criticism is that the 'codes of fair competition' were set by big businesses in their own favour and that they then proceeded to ignore them. There is some truth in this. In 1933, there were 10 000 complaints of code violation. Yet, Badger disputes the amounts of influence big business are credited with having over the NRA. He points out that industries, such as car manufacturing, were already **oligopolies** that had little to gain from the NRA codes and that, when the Supreme Court struck it down in May 1935, the business community did not lament its passing.

Oligopolies: where just a few companies control a whole section of industry.

Did FDR achieve rural recovery?

FDR had much more interest in rural affairs than in industrial issues. He was deeply involved in the Civilian Conservation Corps (CCC), the Tennessee Valley Authority (TVA), the Public Works Administration (PWA) and the Civil Works Administration (CWA). All were considered great New Deal successes.

The CCC, set up in March 1933, gave young men, aged 17 to 25, nine months of work – planting trees, laying telephone lines, managing forests, and so on. They lived in camps and earned $30 per month, of which $25 had to be sent home. This was based on a project FDR had introduced when he was governor of New York State and was very much his own idea. He said:

> 'The idea is to put people to work in the national forests and on other government and state properties.'

It was very important to FDR and the US Government that these young men worked for their wages and were not given handouts. The 'rugged individualism' of the 1920s was still strong in the USA. The army built the camps and military discipline was enforced on the young men. There was a 10 per cent drop-out rate, which was largely due to the military discipline, but the agency remained popular. By August 1933, there were 275 000 men in 1300 camps around the country, which rose to half a million in 2500 camps at its peak at the end of the 1930s. In all, almost three million young men went through the CCC before it ended in 1942.

The TVA, created in May 1933, was based on a plan put forward by Republican Senator George Norris, and was as much about helping farmers as providing jobs and flood relief. Norris had a plan to build dams in the Muscle Shoals area of Alabama to provide power for farmers and jobs in nitrate plants. Twenty dams were built along the Tennessee River to control floods in seven of the poorest states. There was also soil conservation, welfare programmes, fertiliser factories, and so on. The dams provided cheap hydroelectric power in the Tennessee Valley and, along with the Rural Electrification Administration created in 1935, the number of rural homes with electrical power increased from one in 10 to nine in 10. According to Michael J. Heale, in *Franklin D. Roosevelt: The New Deal and War* (1999):

> Probably no other single measure of the New Deal was as responsible for transforming life in the American South.

Senator George Norris (third from right) and various members of Congress from the Tennessee Valley Authority (TVA) region look on as FDR signs the TVA into existence, 18 May 1933. The TVA was one of the largest and most successful of the New Deal agencies.

The CWA, created in November 1933, was crucial in providing jobs during the winter of 1933/4 on various public works. Without this emergency programme many civilians would have starved. When it was clear that public work would be needed for longer, the PWA, which had been set up in June 1933, took over. These agencies built schools, airports, hospitals, bridges, roads and more, and provided jobs for thousands. A total of $3300 million was spent on the PWA alone and, at its peak in the winter of 1933/4, the CWA employed 4.25 million men. Work on the PWA was slow because the projects, such as building airports, were capital intensive. However, the agency built a third of all US hospitals. Altogether, the PWA spent $6 billion on providing a massive boom to the construction industry.

How did farmers benefit from the New Deal?

Farmers got more from FDR and the New Deal than from any other group. FDR wanted to make agriculture more efficient. He wanted to *help* the rural poor, not just bail them out. In March 1933, various agencies were brought together to form the Farm Credit Administration (FCA), which gave relief on mortgages, saving as many as 300 farms a day; and the Commodity Credit Corporation, which gave farmers loans against their crops. According to Ronald Edsforth, in *The New Deal: America's Response to the Great Depression* (2000):

> [These measures] helped to diffuse the farm crisis in the rural regions hit hardest by the Great Depression [and ensured that] traditionally Republican farm states in the Midwest voted for Franklin Roosevelt in the presidential election of 1936.

The Agricultural Adjustment Act 1933 (AAA) was based on Montana's Domestic Allotment Plan, which was a voluntary scheme where farmers were paid to reduce their acreage. Under the AAA, farmers were to group together and set production quotas. In return for cutting production they received a subsidy, from the US Government, which was paid for by a tax on food processing. In 1933, for example, the AAA destroyed 4.5 million acres of cotton but the price rose from 10¢ a pound to 65¢.

By 1941, farm incomes had doubled from their 1932 levels and agricultural debt was reduced by $1 billion. Although agricultural **foreclosures** did not stop, Anthony J. Badger, in *The New Deal: The Depression Years, 1933–1940* (1989), asserts that far more farmers would have lost their land if it had not been for the New Deal.

Foreclosures: when the bank takes back land or property because the mortgage payments have not been met.

Yet, many historians are critical of FDR's agricultural policies. Left-wing writers in the 1960s and 1970s, who were concerned about world hunger, were very critical of a policy that destroyed crops when people were going hungry. Howard Zinn, in *A People's History of the United States* (1980), argues that neither the AAA nor the FCA helped the very poor, such as the **sharecroppers** who made up half of the agricultural population in the 1930s and were living on an average yearly income of $312. Badger, however, argues that FDR could not be too revolutionary because workable radical solutions were not there and what was needed was fast action to deal with the crises.

There is no doubt that farmers saw their standards of living rise in the second half of the decade. However, there is some dispute as to whether FDR should take the credit. It is unclear if the rise in agricultural incomes was due to AAA quotas or the effects of the **dust bowl** in cutting production. Michael Simpson, among others, points out, in *Franklin D. Roosevelt* (1989), that farmers were not spending the money that they received but were saving it in case of future difficulties. By doing this, they were not increasing the demand for industrial goods. At the same time, the taxes on food processing increased the price that urban dwellers had to pay for food. In other words, farmers were doing better at the expense of the urban population. The Supreme Court agreed, in United States versus Butler in 1936, that the AAA was taking money from one group to benefit another and declared the AAA unconstitutional. FDR had to present agricultural subsidies as soil conservation payments; instead of paying the farmers to cut production the Federal Government paid the farmers to conserve the soil by allowing it to lie fallow (unused) until another AAA could be passed in 1938.

Sharecroppers: farmers who work on land owned by someone else. The owner provides the land, seed, and tools in exchange for part of the crops and goods produced on the farm. Many sharecroppers in the 1930s were African-Americans.

Dust bowl: a drought hit the plains of the US in 1934/5 from the Dakotas to Texas. The drought destroyed the topsoil, which was then blown away by the winds.

Did the New Deal reduce poverty and unemployment?

According to Michael Simpson, in *Franklin D. Roosevelt* (1989), the New Deal cannot be judged a tremendous success in reducing poverty and unemployment. He points out that at any one time only one in three Americans was benefiting from a New Deal programme, and each of the programmes had severe limitations. He states:

> [As] thousands of blacks, senior citizens and sharecroppers could testify, the 'forgotten man' often remained forgotten.

However, both he and Ronald Edsforth, in *The New Deal: America's Response to the Great Depression* (2000), emphasise that when judging the New Deal one must take account of the scale of the problem that FDR faced. FDR had to balance the competing interests within the Democratic Party and society. He also believed in a balanced budget, and neither he nor the American public were prepared to spend the amounts of money that would be needed to get the US out of the Depression.

Although the standard view is that the New Deal did not bring about recovery, Edsforth's book, The *New Deal: America's Response to the Great Depression* (2000), gives FDR's performance much more approval. He points out that, although unemployment was still high, the economy was growing until the mid-1930s and would have continued to grow if FDR had not cut spending in 1937. The fact that spending was important in growth was shown in the war when spending ended the Depression. The 1937 budget cut led to a 33 per cent decline in industrial production, a 35 per cent fall in wages and a 13 per cent fall in national income, as well as a rise in unemployment of four million. Edsforth writes:

> As most Americans now know, full employment and dramatic reductions in poverty were not achieved until 1942/3 when 13 million men and women were serving in the armed forces and the United States was supplying huge quantities of war materials and food to its wartime Allies. These facts alone force us to conclude that the New Deal failed to promote real economic recovery; and that it took massive government borrowing, investment and spending during World War II to end the Great Depression. [But] the economic record of the New Deal did not appear dismal to contemporaries.

Contemporaries saw a growth in GNP, a growth in earnings and a fall in unemployment, and for that they thanked FDR.

Did the New Deal 'save' America?

Did the people have faith in the President?

According to historian Ronald Edsforth, in *The New Deal: America's Response to the Great Depression* (2000), American capitalism was in crisis in the early 1930s. Not only was there mass unemployment and the collapse of industry and agriculture but, as Edsforth writes:

> [There was also] daily theft and looting of stores for food, farm strikes, anti-eviction and anti-foreclosure riots, communist-led hunger marches, seizures of public buildings, police gassing and

shooting of unemployed workers, attempted assassinations of public officials, lynch mobs and vigilante violence … .

During FDR's 1932 election campaign, a friend said to him that if the New Deal were a success he would be remembered as the greatest American president. Roosevelt replied that if it were to fail he would be remembered as the last.

In the months between the election and the inauguration, 5000 banks closed, and 20 000 farmers lost their land. Unemployment had reached almost 14 million, and 9 million people had lost their savings. Historians disagree on whether the United States was actually on the verge of collapse but many people at the time felt that this was the case. If nothing else, FDR gave confidence back to the American people. He talked about 'bold persistent experimentation'. 'Try something', he said, 'and if it fails, admit it frankly and try something else.'

The first '100 days' of FDR's first administration saw Congress pass 15 major pieces of legislation to tackle the worst problems of the Depression. After the seeming inaction of the Hoover years, FDR's energy and confidence was crucial in raising morale. People wrote to the President in unheard of numbers: as many as 8000 letters a day were sent to the White House. Millions tuned in to hear his radio broadcasts. He was re-elected in 1936 with a massive 61 per cent of the popular vote and, in spite of problems with the Supreme Court, a recession and a difficult Congress, he was also re-elected for an unprecedented third term in 1940, winning 55 per cent of the votes cast. He won again, for the fourth time, in 1944. It would be hard to dispute that the majority of American people had faith in their president and his leadership.

Was FDR's action on the banks successful?

Action on the banks was crucial to preserving capitalism in the US. Banks were going under at the rate of 40 a day by the time FDR took office. There were $41 billion deposits in US banks but only $6 billion in cash to cover them. In March 1933, the President obtained Congress's permission to close the nation's banks for four days. The so-called 'banking holiday' meant that no more withdrawals could be made and it gave the Federal Government time to act. Under the Emergency Banking Act 1933, FDR used the **Reconstruction Finance Corporation** to assess the viability of banks. It decided that it was necessary for the Federal Government to buy shares in the bank to give it stability. When the banks reopened after the 'banking holiday', the amount of money being put back into accounts was more than

Reconstruction Finance Corporation: established by President Hoover, in February 1932, to give emergency loans to businesses in danger of going bankrupt. In July 1932, it was given the power to lend money to states for poverty relief. FDR took it over when he became president.

the amount being taken out for the first time since the Wall Street crash. FDR had restored people's faith in the banking system. In 1936, there were no bank failures for the first time in 59 years.

FDR also stabilised the New York stock exchange on Wall Street through the creation, in June 1934, of the Securities and Exchange Commission (SEC). Although businessmen at the time resented this interference from the Federal Government, '[they] reluctantly accepted that [it] had brought order to financial markets' (Anthony J. Badger, *The New Deal: The Depression Years, 1933–1940* (1989)). In fact, when President Reagan proposed abolishing the SEC in the 1980s, the New York stock exchange on Wall Street itself objected.

Some historians, notably those on the left, have criticised FDR for not taking the opportunity to **nationalise** the banks. But, as Anthony J. Badger and Michael Simpson point out, this would have led to a long-drawn-out argument with Congress at a time when quick action was essential and when there was no real call for nationalisation. In fact, Hoover had wanted to close the banks in February 1933 and had asked for FDR's cooperation, which was refused. Ronald Edsforth, in *The New Deal: America's Response to the Great Depression* (2000), points out that there were differences in their policies but the real reason was political – FDR did not want Hoover to get the credit if it worked.

Nationalise: to take under government control.

To what extent was America 'saved'?

William E. Leuchtenburg, in *Franklin D. Roosevelt and the New Deal, 1932–1940* (1963), disputes whether FDR 'saved' America. He maintains that, although there was unrest, the people did not want to overthrow the system. The people were angry and bitter but they still believed in American democracy, as shown by the lack of support for extremist parties such as the Communist Party. He argues that the overwhelming emotion in 1932 was apathy. Ronald Edsforth, in *The New Deal: America's Response to the Great Depression* (2000), paints a different picture. He argues that despair affected everyone from poor farmers to millionaires. People did not know which way to turn or how the Depression would end, and there were 'real fears of revolution, or anarchy, or race war, or some awful combination of these'. FDR played down these fears, famously saying that Americans only had to fear 'fear itself' and, by his rapid actions, he restored their confidence in the system and the government.

How radical was the New Deal in protecting working people?

How radical was the '100 days'?

Throughout the 1920s, economists and presidents believed firmly in the necessity of strong financial control and balanced budgets. When the Depression hit, Hoover, and leaders in other countries, believed that if they did not cut spending they would bankrupt their countries. Yet, the New Deal had an average annual deficit of $2.7 billion a year. Was this taking America in a new direction? FDR was, at heart, a **fiscal conservative** like Hoover and his own Treasury Secretary, Henry Morgenthau, but some economists, most notably **John Maynard Keynes**, were arguing that governments should spend their way out of the Depression. FDR was not convinced that **deficit spending** was the answer but he knew that something had to be done and he was prepared to take America into debt in the short term if that was what it took.

During the '100 days', FDR got the Federal Emergency Relief Act (FERA) passed to give money to states to help the poor and unemployed. While this measure was undoubtedly radical in that the Federal Government was stepping into an area that had previously been a state responsibility, the amount given out prevented it from being as successful as it might have been. FERA gave $500 million to feed the poor and unemployed. Half the amount was given as direct federal relief and the other half was made up by the Federal Government giving $1 to match every $3 that the state promised to raise. However, many states cut relief spending knowing that **Harry Hopkins** would have to give them FERA money anyway. Some states

Fiscal conservative: someone who believes in a balanced budget – not spending more than the government gets in taxation.

Deficit financing: government spending more money than it takes in taxation, with the hope that it will increase purchasing power and get the country out of depression.

John Maynard Keynes (1883–1946) Keynes was an influential British economist. As an adviser at the Paris Peace Conference in 1919, he walked out over what he believed were the errors being made over reparation payments. In 1936, he published *The General Theory of Employment, Interest and Money*, which argued for government spending to promote economic stability and recovery from depression. His ideas became widely accepted after World War II until challenged in the 1970s.

Harry Hopkins (1890–1946) Hopkins was a social worker and leading figure in the New Deal. When FDR became president, Hopkins became director of New Deal relief agencies, such as the Federal Emergency Relief Administration, the Civil Works Administration and the Works Progress Administration. He was FDR's leading adviser during World War II and was put in charge of lend-lease.

and cities were unable or unwilling to raise taxes to match the federal funds. And, as Michael Simpson points out, FERA was paid for with money raised from cutting the pay and pensions of federal employees under the Economy Act of March 1933. FDR wanted as much of the New Deal to be as self-financing as possible.

How radical was the Second New Deal?

Efficacy: positive effect.

It seemed that during the Second New Deal (1935–7), FDR had been persuaded of the **efficacy** of federal spending. The Works Progress Administration (WPA), set up in April 1935, was originally allocated just under $2 billion for relief and public works, yet ended up spending more than $5 billion, becoming the most important New Deal agency. Rather than conversion to a more radical Keynesian policy, FDR was acting in response to riots, in the winter of 1934, protesting at the slow progress of recovery, and he continued to believe in the desirability of a balanced budget. In 1937, he became concerned by the rising deficit and cut spending by over $1 billion. Unemployment shot up to 10.2 million and FDR had to ask Congress once again for money for public works.

The WPA was, at the time, one of the more controversial elements of the New Deal. Although public works money had been given to artists and writers in other programmes, there had been nothing to match the scale of the WPA. The WPA paid out $4.8 billion, funding artists to paint murals in public buildings, the Federal Theatre Project to take plays on tours of the USA and the Federal Writers' Project to produce a set of guides for each of the 48 states. It was also

An artist painting a mural as part of a WPA initiative. The WPA received much criticism for employing actors, writers and painters, but their work brought art to the masses and can still be seen in many American cities today.

the New Deal agency that gave most help to groups previously ignored, including African-Americans and women. Although it only reached a third of those in need, the WPA showed how federal money could be used imaginatively. It moved Federal Government into the arts, which continued under President Johnson with the creation of the National Endowment for the Arts. Critics, at the time and since, have debated whether it is the government's job to subsidise the arts. However, the WPA made the arts accessible to the lower classes. The Federal Theatre Project, for example, allowed poor people to see theatrical productions for the first time in their lives.

Also, in 1935, the National Labor Relations Act (or Wagner Act) gave legal rights and protection to trade unions for the first time, allowing them to grow and to represent the ordinary worker. Historians Michael Simpson and Patrick Maney argue that the Act was entirely the work of Senator Robert Wagner and that FDR even considered vetoing it. On the other hand, Michael J. Heale, in *Franklin D. Roosevelt: The New Deal and War* (1999), argues that the Act only received such a speedy passage through Congress because FDR put his weight behind it. Whatever the case, the Act spurred a massive growth in union membership. In 1935, the Congress of Industrial Organisations was formed to represent semi-skilled and un-skilled workers, including women and black people. Trade union membership grew from just under three million in 1930 to almost nine million in 1940. It continued to grow throughout World War II when the labour shortage put ordinary workers in a much more powerful position. By 1950, there were 15 million members. Labour laws also strengthened the link between workers and the Democratic Party, and by 1940 the unions were the biggest contributors to Democratic Party funds.

The Social Security Act, according to Carl N. Degler, in *Out of Our Past* (1984), was a 'revolutionary' measure. This was not designed to deal with the immediate problems but designed to ensure that, in the future, no economic recession could have the same devastating effects on people's lives as the Depression, which had left millions with no income. Wisconsin State was the only state that had any form of unemployment insurance when the stock exchange crash hit in 1929. US states were totally unprepared to deal with mass unemployment, so FDR aimed to provide Americans with a basic welfare system. He introduced: pensions for the over-65s financed by a payroll tax; unemployment benefit paid for by a tax on employers (who during the New Deal got a rebate for not laying people off); and categorical assistance to those who could not work (for example disability benefit paid for by federal and state funds). The United

States lagged well behind other developed countries in introducing a welfare system. Britain had had similar programmes since 1911, and Bismarck had introduced social security in Germany as early as the 1880s.

At the time, there were many criticisms of the Social Security Act. Knowing that pensions would not be due until 1940, **Progressives** argued that the people needed the money immediately. They also argued that increasing taxes on employers and employees would reduce spending at a time when spending needed to go up. Also, left-wing critics disapproved of the lack of health insurance in the Act. Above all, there were major discrepancies. In Arkansas, for example, families got $8.10 for each dependent child, whereas in Massachusetts it was $61.07.

Progressives: people who believe that the government should use its power for social reform.

However, in FDR's defence, he had to give the states a role within social security to get the Act through Congress. As Anthony J. Badger points out, in *The New Deal: The Depression Years, 1933–1940* (1989), the Federal Government had neither the manpower nor the structures for such a massive programme. FDR was dependent on the states for the implementation of the policy. His insistence on funding social security from taxation was so that people would feel that they had contributed to it and so would not allow future politicians to cut it. FDR would have had to fight Congress and the American Medical Association to get healthcare included in the Act. The New Dealers were fully aware of the weaknesses of the Social Security Act but they felt that additions and improvements could be added later. The important thing was to make a start.

Assessment

The social policies of the Second New Deal do seem to portray a government moving in a more radical and left-wing way. Arthur M. Schlesinger Jr. is one historian who, in *The Imperial Presidency* (1973), argues that there was a definite shift in policy, but William E. Leuchtenburg, in *Franklin D. Roosevelt and the New Deal, 1932–1940* (1963), maintains that it was a change of emphasis rather than a change of direction. He points out that many of the measures had been 'in the works' for a while and it was simply due to timing that they were passed in 1935.

Most historians agree that FDR had no coherent ideology, but Ronald Edsforth, in *The New Deal: America's Response to the Great Depression* (2000), says that the New Deal had an ideological commitment to economic security for every American citizen. In his 'fireside chat' on 11 January 1944, FDR talked about an Economic Bill of Rights that planned to provide every American citizen with access to a job, a decent home, food, clothing, education, and protection in old age, sickness and unemployment. However, Patrick J. Maney, in *The Roosevelt Presence: The Life and Legacy of FDR* (1992), argues that FDR believed that the capitalist system would put this in place and that the Federal Government would only need to step in to fill in the gaps. He writes:

> Yet in subsequent speeches, it became clear that Roosevelt envisaged no great expansion of government. He seemed confident that the free enterprise system would be able to make the Economic Bill of Rights a reality, with government limiting itself to a supporting role.

World War II and FDR's death, in 1945, prevented this from happening, but the ideas were to become dominant in the Democratic Party for the next 20 years.

Left-wing historian Howard Zinn, however, is much more critical of how much the New Deal changed things. In *A People's History of the United States* (1980), he states:

> Enough help had been given to enough people to make Roosevelt a hero to millions, but the same system that had brought depression and crisis – the system of waste, of inequality, of concern for profit over human need – remained.

New Deal: success or failure?

1. Read the following extract and answer the question.

   'This is truly legislation in the interests of national welfare. We must recognise that if we are to maintain a healthy economy and thriving production, we need to maintain the standard of living of the lower income groups of our population who constitute 90 per cent of our purchasing power.'

   (From a speech, given in September 1935, by Frances Perkins on the Social Security Act. Frances Perkins was the first female Cabinet minister in US history. She was appointed by FDR, in 1933, as Secretary of Labor.)

   Using the information in the extract above, and from this section, explain the reasons for the passing of the Social Security Act.

2. To what extent did the New Deal improve 'the standard of living of the lower income groups'?

2

Was FDR's foreign policy isolationist or interventionist?

What were FDR's foreign policy beliefs?

To what extent did FDR pursue an isolationist policy towards Europe and Japan?

Framework of events

1932	FDR elected thirty-second president of United States
1933	Hitler comes to power in Germany
	FDR establishes diplomatic relations with USSR
1935	Neutrality Act prohibits export of US arms to belligerents
1936	Neutrality Act prohibits loans to belligerents
	FDR elected for second term
	Nye Committee Report
1937	Neutrality Act bans Americans from travelling on ships of belligerent nations
	Japanese attack on Nanking
	FDR makes Chicago speech
1938	Munich Agreement between Britain and Germany
1939	Outbreak of war in Europe; FDR declares 'limited national emergency'
1940	Selective Training and Service Act introduces conscription
	Destroyer Deal, trading 50 ships for British colonial territory
	FDR elected for third term
1941	Lend-Lease Act
	Attack on USS *Greer*
	Atlantic Charter agreed
	Japanese attack on Pearl Harbor
1943	FDR, Churchill and Stalin meet at Teheran to map out strategy
1944	FDR elected for fourth term
1945	Meeting at Yalta by 'Big Three' to discuss post-war world

---

Landmark Study   The book that changed people's views

Robert Dallek, *Franklin D. Roosevelt and American Foreign Policy, 1932–1945* (OUP, 1995)

Dallek presents FDR as an internationalist due to his background and temperament. According to Dallek, FDR believed that peace and prosperity were essential to each other and that the US had a role to play in the establishment of both. He also points out the constraints under which FDR worked, due to the problems at home during the Depression and the isolationism of the American public. He believes that FDR made mistakes but was largely successful in achieving his foreign policy aims.

Dallek's prize-winning book concentrates on FDR's foreign policy in its own right rather than as an afterthought to the New Deal. This detailed book convincingly defends FDR against the criticisms that other historians have made of his handling of foreign affairs.

THE United States in the 1920s followed a policy of isolationism, attempting to stay out of the affairs of European countries. The US did not want to get pulled into another war as it had been in 1917. Yet, under FDR's presidency, the United States did in fact find itself in another war; one much longer and more destructive than the first. Why did this happen? Was FDR an interventionist, who pursued an active foreign policy with the intention of supporting the Allies all along, or was he honestly attempting to keep the US free from entanglement in Europe and the Far East?

Some historians, such as William E. Leuchtenburg, in *Franklin D. Roosevelt and the New Deal, 1932–1940* (1963), argue that FDR hoped to keep the US out of the war but that he did not really know how to respond to events in Europe and the Far East. These historians believe that FDR intended to give material support to the Allies in the event of war but he did not intend for the US to send troops to fight in Europe. Others argue that, far from trying to maintain an isolationist stance, FDR went so far as to manipulate events to ensure America's entry into the war. Thomas Fleming, in *The War Within World War II* (2001), for example, argues that the Roosevelt administration purposefully leaked a secret report planning to send to Europe a five-million-man army. This leak prompted Hitler to fear American involvement, and he declared war on the USA. Others, such as Robert Dallek, in *Franklin D. Roosevelt and American Foreign Policy, 1932–1945* (1995) (see **Landmark Study** above), argue that FDR was an interventionist but in the sense that he felt he could influence events and *prevent* war by taking an active role in foreign policy.

In many ways it is difficult to say what FDR's beliefs were regarding isolationism and interventionism. He always played his cards close to his chest, and even men who worked closely with him throughout his career were never sure exactly what he believed in.

What were FDR's foreign policy beliefs?

FDR's upbringing and long-held interest in foreign affairs

It is clear that, although domestic economic pressures brought FDR to office, he had a long-held interest in foreign affairs. Robert Dallek, in *Franklin D. Roosevelt and American Foreign Policy, 1932–1945* (1995), points out:

Cosmopolitan: having knowledge and understanding of foreign places and customs.

> Aside from his [fifth] cousin Theodore, Franklin D. Roosevelt was the most **cosmopolitan** American to enter the White House since John Quincy Adams in 1825.

Throughout FDR's childhood, his family took regular holidays in Europe, and he was taught to speak both French and German. As a young man, he continued to travel, visiting the Caribbean and cycling through Holland and Germany. At Groton School, he joined the missionary society and took part in several debates on foreign affairs.

FDR as nationalist

FDR's political hero was his fifth cousin Theodore Roosevelt. Theodore Roosevelt was a skilful politician, who believed that the United States should play an active role in world affairs. FDR actively copied his cousin's career, becoming Assistant Secretary of the Navy in 1913. This was a position that Theodore Roosevelt had held in 1897/8. In this post, FDR argued that the US should have a 'big navy' to allow it to meet any threats to its security, and to allow it to pursue an active policy around the world for the benefit of the American people and of other countries. (These beliefs often led to conflict between FDR and his superior – Secretary of the Navy Josephus Daniels.)

While as Assistant Secretary of the Navy, FDR supported the Preparedness Movement, which argued for the need for the United States to prepare its military and economy more effectively should the country find itself having to join in the war that was looming in Europe. FDR argued, for example, that the navy, army and State Departments should form a Council of National Defense to coordinate military policy. When the US did join the war, FDR gained a reputation as an extremely capable administrator.

FDR as internationalist

As well as supporting Theodore Roosevelt's nationalist concept of America's role in the world, Patrick J. Maney, in *The Roosevelt Presence: The Life and Legacy of FDR* (1992), argues that Franklin was also an internationalist like Woodrow Wilson.

FDR strongly supported US involvement in the League of Nations, believing that the League would make rearmament unnecessary and war less likely. Robert Dallek, in *Franklin D, Roosevelt and American Foreign Policy, 1932–1945* (1995), however, sees this support of the League as more opportunistic; Wilson was immensely popular immediately after World War I and allying himself with this policy would advance FDR's political career. However, even when the public turned against the League and the Senate refused to ratify American membership, FDR continued to believe that active engagement in the League was the best way to protect American interests. According to Michael Simpson, in *Franklin D. Roosevelt* (1989):

> By the time he left office, he was developing a more responsible attitude to war and peace and a positive conception of America's global role.

When FDR became president, the mood of the United States was distinctly against foreign adventures. But, according to Michael Simpson, FDR remained convinced that the US had a role to play in defending democracy and human rights, especially in the face of the growing threat from fascism. Unlike most New Dealers, FDR was not an isolationist; instead he believed that the best way to prevent war was to intervene in international affairs, not avoid them. When war did come, he felt that giving the British moral and material support would mean they could win without the need for American military action (what William E. Leuchtenburg calls being a 'grand neutral'), and even if military action were needed it would require no more than naval and air support. FDR did not foresee the US having to support the Allied cause with American troops.

Contradictory policies

Lobbying by arms manufacturers: pressure put on the government, by weapons manufacturers, to take a more active foreign policy and build up the country's military.

Despite FDR's internationalist outlook, he also worked hard to ensure American neutrality throughout the 1930s. He seemed to agree with the findings of the Nye Committee, whose report in 1936 argued that **lobbying by arms manufacturers** had pushed the US into World War I. FDR also supported neutrality legislation and worked hard to ensure that the US did not become embroiled in the Spanish Civil War. With regard to Latin America, FDR announced as early as 1933 that the US would pursue a Good Neighbour Policy and would not intervene in the affairs of Latin American states. This promise was confirmed at the Pan-American Conference later in the year, and put into practice when US troops were removed from Haiti and the Dominican Republic. In 1936, when the New Mexican Government nationalised US owned oil companies, Roosevelt looked for a compensation deal instead of confrontation. Yet, at the same time, a visit by an American warship to Cuba, in 1934, was instrumental in helping rebels overthrow the democratic rule of Grau San Martín and replace it with the dictatorship of Fulgencio Batista. And, in both Nicaragua and the Dominican Republic, American-trained soldiers helped dictators like Somoza and Trujillo remain in power. To some, it seemed that the US was prepared to be a 'good neighbour' so long as governments remained pro-American.

FDR's policies, throughout the 1930s, seemed frequently to be contradictory. William E. Leuchtenburg, in *Franklin D. Roosevelt and the New Deal, 1932–1940* (1963), says that FDR was deeply troubled by the events in Europe but did not know what to do for the best. Robert Dallek, in *Franklin D. Roosevelt and American Foreign Policy, 1932–1945* (1995), places more emphasis on the domestic constraints under which FDR operated. He recognises that for FDR to achieve what he wanted at home, he needed the support of Congress and had to go along with a Congressional desire for a passive foreign policy.

To what extent did FDR pursue an isolationist policy towards Europe and Japan?

Isolationism and the public's needs

Two months before FDR took his oath of office, Adolf Hitler came to power in Germany in January 1933. Fascism was on the rise throughout Europe in Italy, Germany and Spain, yet foreign policy experts in the US were telling the President that there would be no war. If there were to be a war, FDR knew how inadequately prepared the United States was. The US had an army the size of Sweden, an industry in deep depression, and a military so poorly equipped that, when America did finally go to war, US troops were initially training with cardboard weapons. If nothing else, these considerations limited FDR's ability to pursue an interventionist foreign policy.

FDR was also highly aware of the mood of the American public. The events of World War I were still strong in people's memories. The losses and seeming futility of that conflict had led America, in the 1920s, to adopt a foreign policy of isolationism. As many historians have shown, this isolationism was only partial. In the 1920s, the USA had not supported the League of Nations and had taken no action when Japan invaded Manchuria. However, the USA had participated in world trade, developed the **Dawes Plan**, attended the League-sponsored disarmament conference and the Washington naval conference, and signed the **Kellogg-Briand Pact** outlawing war. However, isolationism was a belief strongly held and supported by the public and, therefore, a belief FDR could not ignore.

During the election, and in a speech in 1933, FDR asserted his belief that the USA should remain free from foreign entanglements. William E. Leuchtenburg, in *Franklin D. Roosevelt and the New Deal 1932–1940* (1963), puts FDR's protestations down to the need for support from the news media rather than a sincerely held belief. The publication of the Nye Committee Report in 1936, however, strengthened support for an isolationist stand. As late as 1937, Indiana Congressman Louis Ludlow put forward a constitutional amendment to require a referendum before the President could declare war. The measure was defeated in the House of Representatives but, in spite of FDR strenuously arguing that the amendment would tie the hands of any president, 209 members voted in favour. The narrowness of the vote convinced FDR that the nation still 'wanted peace' and, according to William Leuchtenburg, shows how tenuous FDR's control of foreign policy was.

Dawes Plan: signed in 1924, this was the agreement, between the USA, France, Britain, Belgium and Germany, for the rescheduling of the reparations payments that Germany owed at the end of World War I. Germany's refusal to pay its instalment in 1922 had led to an invasion by the French and Belgians in 1923. The American Government came up with the Dawes Plan to try to resolve the situation and prevent the outbreak of another war.

Kellog-Briand Pact: the agreement made in 1928, signed by 65 nations, outlawing war as a method of policy.

The Neutrality Acts

The support for isolation, was translated into the Neutrality Acts of 1935, 1936 and 1937. These Acts respectively provided for an **arms embargo** against warring nations, the prohibition of loans to **belligerents**, and a ban on US citizens travelling on the ships of belligerent nations. Robert Dallek, in *Franklin D. Roosevelt and American Foreign Policy, 1932–1945* (1995), states that FDR pushed for a more flexible measure in 1935 that would give him the power to decide who was and who was not a belligerent. Congress rejected the idea and, because FDR needed their support for his domestic programmes, he was unable to achieve a modification of the legislation.

Arms embargo: prohibition of the sale of arms to a country to try to get it to stop fighting.

Belligerents: those actively involved in war or conflict.

Americans continued to fear that the European nations would drag them into a war. The invasion of Ethiopia by the Italian army, and the outbreak of civil war in Spain, confirmed the belief among many Americans of the necessity of the Neutrality Acts, which were even extended in January 1937 to cover civil wars. According to William E. Leuchtenburg, this was done with FDR's support. Michael Simpson, in *Franklin D. Roosevelt* (1989), feels that FDR failed to support those senators wanting to give help to the Spanish republicans, not because he wished to but because he did not feel the American public was ready to support the change. According to Michael J. Heale, in *Franklin D. Roosevelt: The New Deal and War* (1999):

> [FDR] blamed the neutrality laws for encouraging fascist aggression, but Congress was loath to amend them.

Did FDR's policy change with the build-up to war?

FDR making his 'quarantine' speech in Chicago, 5 October 1937. He warned of increased world lawlessness caused by the violation of agreements and treaties, international aggression and lack of respect for the rights and freedom of others.

In 1936, the Nazi army moved into the Rhineland, breaking the terms of the Treaty of Versailles. In the Far East, Japan continued to expand its territory and, in 1937, attacked the Chinese city of Nanking, massacring thousands of its inhabitants.

On 5 October 1937, FDR made a speech in Chicago in which he spoke of the epidemic of lawlessness around the world. He said that America had to oppose this trend and 'quarantine' those nations responsible for the epidemic. The speech caused a stir at the time as to exactly what FDR meant. Robert Dallek, in *Franklin D. Roosevelt and American Foreign Policy, 1932–1945* (1995), maintains that

FDR was doing nothing more than warning the American people that as the world became more 'lawless' they too could be in danger. Dallek believes that the President was not trying to institute a change of policy, such as the introduction of a policy of sanctions against Japan, or persuade the people of the need for such a change. Likewise, William Leuchtenburg, in *Franklin D. Roosevelt and the New Deal, 1932–1940* (1963), points out that FDR was at pains to say that he was not referring to some kind of trade embargo, and that the speech is not evidence that FDR was an internationalist. However, Patrick J. Maney, in *The Roosevelt Presence: The Life and Legacy of FDR* (1992), says it is still not clear what FDR meant when he talked about the 'quarantine' of aggressors and, certainly at the time, some saw the speech as heralding a change in US policy. If, as some historians suggest, FDR made the speech to test public support for a more interventionist foreign policy, he got his answer when he was threatened with **impeachment**.

Impeachment: to remove the president from office and put him on trial.

It was not only Americans who wished to avoid war. In September 1938, British Prime Minister Neville Chamberlain travelled to Munich to talk to Hitler to try to avert a crisis over Czechoslovakia. Chamberlain returned to Britain claiming to have achieved peace, but it was at the expense of giving a large chunk of Czech territory – the Sudetenland – to the Nazis. FDR telegraphed Chamberlain, calling him a 'good man' for agreeing to meet Hitler. Patrick Maney and William Leuchtenburg both say that FDR supported the agreement and Chamberlain's policy of **appeasement**. Michael Simpson, however, says that FDR was very angry at the outcome of the conference and believed it only delayed war. Eleanor Roosevelt said that FDR opposed the agreement in private but did not say so in public. FDR's actions after the conference indicate that he saw the emergence of German power as of great consequence to the US. He pushed Congress for an expanded air force and a naval build-up. He also wanted to sell planes to the French, but public hostility and the Neutrality Acts prevented this. He did, however, initiate secret military talks between Britain, France and the USA.

Appeasement: British policy in the 1930s to avoid war with Germany by giving in to Hitler's 'reasonable' demands.

Did FDR remain 'neutral' with the onset of war?

When war did come, in September 1939, FDR immediately made it clear to the American people that he intended to remain neutral. However, in his 'fireside chat' on 3 September he famously said that 'even a neutral cannot be asked to close his mind or his conscience'. In *Franklin D. Roosevelt and American Foreign Policy, 1932–1945* (1995), Robert Dallek states:

[To FDR] morality and self-interest … compelled America to aid Britain and France: the preservation of American values and national peace depended on the defeat of Berlin.

Like the American public, FDR wanted to stay out of Europe's war, but he believed the best way to do this was to support the Allied cause. Polls showed that the public supported Britain and that the majority of Americans wanted the US to supply arms but not get involved. Some, however, opposed FDR's view and argued, somewhat cynically, that if Germany won it would leave the US in control of the western hemisphere. In *The Roosevelt Presence: The Life and Legacy of FDR* (1992), Patrick J. Maney criticises FDR for attacking these people instead of educating them to his own view. He also points out that FDR treated those who opposed him like enemies. He even had their phones tapped.

In the election in November, FDR had to be wary of Republican attacks and so promised not to send 'our boys' to fight in Europe. The fall of France had made the American public more supportive of FDR's policies and more willing to give material aid to the Allies, but divisions remained strong. 1940 saw the creation of both the internationalist Committee to Defend America by Aiding the Allies (CDAAA) and the isolationist America First Committee (AFC). FDR strengthened his position by taking two Republicans into the Cabinet – Henry Stimson as Secretary of War and Frank Knox as Secretary of the Navy. With their support, and support from veteran groups, FDR was able to get Congress to pass the Selective Service Act. This was America's first ever peacetime draft, making men aged 21 to 45 years old eligible for one year of military service and providing $500 000 million for defence. Veteran organisations supported the Act, but William E. Leuchtenburg, in *Franklin D. Roosevelt and the New Deal* (1963), says the measure was **Conscripts**: men called up by the government to serve in the military. opposed by the military, who believed that **conscripts** would weaken the regular army.

FDR still saw this measure as a precaution. He believed that the best way for the US to avoid war was to provide support to the Allies to strengthen their ability to fight and defeat the Nazis. The Neutrality Acts, however, made this difficult. FDR proposed to amend them to allow Britain to buy arms, which they would have to carry in their own ships to avoid American ships becoming targets. He talked carefully to both Republican and Democrat representatives **Bipartisan**: having the support of both the Republican and Democratic Parties. to ensure **bipartisan** support and, according to Dallek, FDR was able to persuade Congress to pass this 'cash and carry' measure by presenting it as a strategy to keep the United States out of the war.

Did FDR's actions tie the US more tightly to the Allied cause?

FDR's critics believed that the President's actions were tying the US more and more tightly to the Allied cause. Criticism increased with the Destroyer Deal of 1940 and the Lend-Lease Act of 1941.

In 1940, the US exchanged 50 old destroyers in return for British colonial territory where the US could develop bases. William E. Leuchtenburg, Michael Simpson and Michael J. Heale all emphasise how FDR **circumvented** Congress over the deal. Leuchtenburg asserts that FDR did this because he knew that if he did not he would fail to get their support. If the rise of Nazism was the threat to the US that FDR asserted it was, then why, congressmen asked, was the President giving away ships that might be needed to defend America? Once again FDR 'sold' the deal to the public by saying it was in America's interest to help Britain. He said the deal was the most important defence measure for the US since the **Louisiana Purchase**. Having bases around the world would enable the US to protect its interests more effectively, and the destroyers would allow Britain to continue its fight against fascism.

In spite of the help given by the United States, by the spring of 1941 Churchill was warning FDR that Britain could no longer afford the arms it needed to continue the war. On 11 March 1941, Congress passed the Lend-Lease Act. This gave Britain arms and supplies that would be returned or paid for after the war. Over the next four years Britain received $50 billion worth of supplies. By claiming that the assets were being loaned or leased, FDR got around the terms of the Neutrality Acts. FDR again presented the measure as essential to US defence. He likened it to lending your neighbour a garden hose because their house is on fire – if you refused or made them buy their own hose your house could burn down too. In his 'fireside chat' at the end of December 1940, FDR had emphasised the danger to America if Britain lost the war. He said that the Americans would find themselves living at the point of a gun. He once again emphasised that the best way to avoid war was to become 'the great arsenal of democracy'. In *Franklin D. Roosevelt and American Foreign Policy, 1932–1945* (1995), Robert Dallek says it was one of the most successful speeches that FDR ever gave and, in spite of protests in New York and Washington against lend-lease, opinion polls showed an 80 per cent approval of the speech.

Although FDR presented lend-lease as a defence measure, Michael J. Heale says that it was the greatest commitment the President could make to the Allied cause short of war. In *Franklin D. Roosevelt* (1989),

Circumvented: by-passed the power of Congress and used the Executive power of the President.

Louisiana Purchase: in 1803, the US bought, from the French, an area between the Rocky Mountains and the Mississippi River. It cost $15 million but added the whole of the Mississippi Valley to the United States.

Michael Simpson asserts that FDR himself acknowledged this view. FDR seemed to be making good the promise he had made in Virginia during the election campaign to 'extend to the opponents of force the material resources of [the] nation'.

Did FDR fully intend to go to war?

FDR does appear to have gone beyond simply supplying material resources to the British. In the Atlantic, attacks by German U-boats were having a devastating effect on British shipping. In 1941, 1500 ships were sunk. FDR gave secret instructions to the US navy to escort British ships crossing the Atlantic. He also announced an extension of America's security zone as far north as Greenland, although he refused to provide the convoys Churchill asked for. The navy ships escorting the British vessels had been given permission by FDR to fire at German ships if necessary and, in September, an incident occurred that seemed it might lead to war.

On 4 September 1941, a British plane and the USS *Greer* spotted a U-boat and gave chase. The plane dropped depth charges and the U-boat fired a torpedo at the ship. The USS *Greer,* in turn, dropped depth charges, and more torpedoes were fired. Neither vessel was sunk in the chase, and the navy told the President that the Germans probably did not know the ship's nationality. FDR, however, told the public that the Germans knew it was an American ship and that the Germans fired first. Michael Simpson, in *Franklin D. Roosevelt* (1989), sees this as hypocrisy, saying that FDR talked about peace while he courted war. In *Franklin D. Roosevelt and American Foreign Policy, 1932–1945* (1995), Robert Dallek justifies FDR's deception and blames the American public who, at the time, wanted to defeat Hitler but did not want to go to war to do it. He says:

> In the light of the national unwillingness to face up fully to the international dangers confronting the country, it is difficult to fault Roosevelt for building a consensus by devious means.

Dallek believes that, by the spring of 1941, FDR had come to believe that the US would have to fight but that if he waited the Allies would be weaker. Although Dallek defends FDR's lies as being in the national interest, even he admits this did set a dangerous precedent for future leaders to mislead the public in time of war.

Some of FDR's opponents believed the USS *Greer* incident was manufactured to create the pretext for war. Certainly, Secretary of War Henry Stimson advised FDR to do more to help the British and argued that the summer and autumn of 1941 was a good time to act as the Germans were tied up with their invasion of the USSR.

Patrick J. Maney is not convinced that FDR's policies were a pretext for war. As he points out, in *The Roosevelt Presence: The Life and Legacy of FDR* (1992), polls showed that three out of five people believed it was more important to defeat Germany than to stay out of the war. If he had wanted to, FDR could have used the USS *Greer* incident as a way to persuade the public to go to war with Nazi Germany, but he did not. Yet, in the August, FDR had met with Churchill just off the coast of Newfoundland, and Churchill had come away from the meeting convinced that FDR would manufacture an incident to take America into the war. Also, at the meeting, the two men issued a set of principles that became known as the Atlantic Charter. These principles included arms reduction, self-determination, freedom of the seas, free trade, and so on. As Michael J. Heale, in *Franklin D Roosevelt: The New Deal and War* (1999), points out; the Atlantic Charter was a list of war aims issued by a country that was not at war.

After the incident with the USS *Greer*, FDR gave US navy ships permission to sink German ships on sight. The Americans were in the war in the Atlantic in all but name. If FDR had indeed come around to the view that America would have to fight, it is possible that he would have joined the Allied cause. In the end, however, it was the Japanese not the Germans who made him make that decision.

Did FDR invite the attack on Pearl Harbor?

Moralistic: believing and acting as though you are in the right when it is not necessarily the case.

According to Michael Simpson, in *Franklin D. Roosevelt* (1989), American policy with regard to the Far East was muddled and **moralistic** in the 1930s. On the one hand, the American public and the administration saw the rise of fascism in Europe and in the Far East as intimately connected but, on the other hand, Japan was seen as different from Germany. While the public wanted to avoid war in the East, as they did in Europe, many felt war with Japan was inevitable. While isolationism was largely seen as a policy towards Europe, the public still did not want FDR taking US troops to fight in the East. To prevent war, FDR tried to work with moderate Japanese leaders. At the same time, he tried to send messages that would halt Japanese expansion. Unfortunately those messages were not always understood; by taking small measures against the Japanese, the hard-liners in Japan's Government believed that FDR did not have the will to act.

According to Michael Simpson, in *Franklin D. Roosevelt* (1989),

Great power: a state that, through a mix of economic, military and political power, has a lot of influence on other states.

FDR was obsessed with China's **great power** status. He hoped that, with American support, China would develop into a democratic nation and be a beacon for the rest of Asia. A strong China would also act as a block on Japanese expansion. Patrick J. Maney, in *The Roosevelt Presence: The Life and Legacy of FDR* (1992), points out that, in fact, the US did more trade with Japan than it did with China. When Japan attacked China in 1937 and massacred the people of the city of Nanking, the US took little action. In fact, the US administration argued that no state of war existed between China and Japan, so the Neutrality Acts did not apply and the US could continue to send supplies to **Chiang Kai-Shek**. This double standard led some critics to argue that FDR was hoping to provoke Japan. According to Michael Parrish, in *Anxious Decades: America in Prosperity and Depression, 1920–1941* (1992), the policy encouraged Chiang Kai-Shek to believe he had US support and made him less willing to negotiate with Japan.

It was shortly after the attack on China that FDR made his Chicago speech (5 October 1937) condemning lawless nations. To some it seemed that FDR was moving away from isolationism, but FDR still hoped to work with moderate Japanese leaders to avoid war. However, Howard Zinn, in *A People's History of the United States* (1980), criticises American inaction over Nanking, saying that America did nothing about the massacre and only acted when its economic interests were at stake. Michael Simpson, however, argues that the American public was not ready for war, and that when the Japanese sank USS *Panay* there was great relief when the Japanese apologised and offered compensation.

As Japan continued to expand aggressively into Dutch and French territory, the American Government was divided on how to act. According to Patrick Maney, in *The Roosevelt Presence: The Life and Legacy of FDR* (1992), FDR saw the issue in a European context – Britain's ability to fight the Nazis might be impeded by its need to defend its colonies in the East. FDR continued to negotiate, but he cut off supplies of scrap metal and sent the Pacific fleet to the base at Pearl Harbor. Some historians have seen these moves, and

Chiang Kai-Shek (1887–1975)
Chiang Kai-Shek was a soldier, a politician and a revolutionary. In 1928, he became the leader of the Chinese Nationalist Movement and helped to defeat the Manchu dynasty and establish a new republican government in China. He fought against the Japanese during World War II but, after the war, his Nationalists fought and lost a civil war to Mao Zedong's Chinese Communist Party. In 1949, he and his followers fled to Taiwan, which became a strong ally of the US and, until 1971, held the Chinese seat on the United Nations Security Council. Chiang Kai-Shek became president of Taiwan in 1949 until his death.

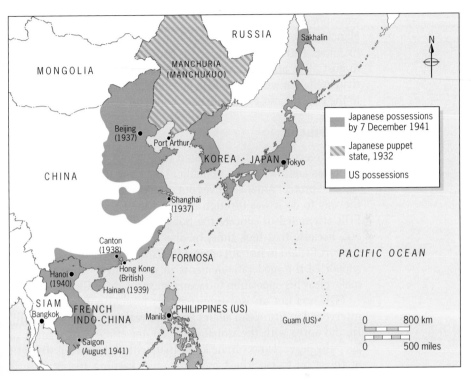

RUSSIA
Sakhalin

MONGOLIA

MANCHURIA
(MANCHUKUO)

Beijing
(1937)
Port Arthur

KOREA · JAPAN · Tokyo

CHINA

Shanghai
(1937)

Japanese possessions
by 7 December 1941

Japanese puppet
state, 1932

US possessions

Canton
(1938)

FORMOSA

PACIFIC OCEAN

Hanoi ·
(1940)
Hong Kong
(British)
Hainan (1939)

SIAM
Bangkok ·
FRENCH
INDO-CHINA
Manila

PHILIPPINES (US)

Guam (US)

Saigon
(August 1941)

0   800 km

0   500 miles

Japanese expansion until
1941.

the subsequent oil embargo, as moves to invite an attack on the Pacific fleet, giving FDR the excuse for war. Michael Heale, Patrick Maney and Robert Dallek refute this. They believe that FDR's aim was to show the Japanese how serious he was and hopefully force them to back down. James T. Patterson, in *America in the Twentieth Century* (1994), also argues in favour of FDR's policies, saying that their advantage was that they were restrained and incremental.

FDR was still keen to avert war with Japan as he seemed to be moving closer to war in Europe, and he did not want war on two fronts. However, the Japanese saw the oil embargo as a potentially fatal blow to their ability to fight. They believed they had to attack first and defeat the US before they were no longer able to do so. This is why they launched a surprise attack on Pearl Harbor. Patrick Maney, in *The Roosevelt Presence: The Life and Legacy of FDR* (1992), states:

> No persuasive evidence has ever surfaced to suggest that, as some people suspected, Roosevelt knew in advance of the attack on Pearl Harbor but allowed it to proceed in order to bring a reluctant nation into the war against Germany.

Nevertheless, both sides continued to negotiate into October and

November 1941. They failed, however, to agree on the status of Manchuria, on withdrawal from China, and on sanctions. According to James Patterson, the Japanese had decided on war as early as August 1941 and nothing FDR did would have avoided it. Rather than invite war with Japan, FDR had done all he could to avoid it but, in the end, the most he could have hoped for was to postpone it.

Assessment

FDR's freedom to act was limited throughout the 1930s by both Congress and the American public. Like them, he wanted to avoid war and protect American lives but, unlike many, he did not believe the way to do it was through isolating the US from world affairs. FDR attempted to educate the public to the dangers facing them but, because that took time, he also took what steps he could to support Britain in its fight against fascism. With regard to Japan, he supported the moderate elements in government while trying to make clear his opposition to Japanese expansion in China.

FDR was not an isolationist in his foreign policy; he clearly intervened in European affairs and gave real support to Churchill. He did agree with the isolationists on one thing – he wanted to keep the peace. However, he knew that, with the growing strength of those he called 'the bandit nations', keeping the peace was increasingly unlikely.

Was FDR's foreign policy isolationist or interventionist?

1. Read the following extract about FDR's 'quarantine' speech, and answer the question.

   'In the fall of 1937 he appeared to edge cautiously away from non-involvement ... At last, so it seemed, Roosevelt was moving toward a policy of resistance.'

   (J.T. Patterson, *America in the Twentieth Century*, Harcourt Brace, 1994.)

   Using the information in the extract above, and from this section, explain to what extent you agree that FDR's speech in Chicago, 1937, marked a turning point in his foreign policy.

2. 'For the first five years of his presidency, FDR steered cautiously between isolationism and interventionalism.' How far do you agree with this view of FDR's foreign policy?

3

Was FDR the first imperial president?

> ### How did FDR expand presidential power in domestic politics?

> ### How did FDR expand presidential power in foreign affairs?

Framework of events

1932	FDR elected thirty-second president of United States
1933	The '100 days'
	Announcement of Good Neighbour Policy
1934	Formation of American Liberty League
1935	Second New Deal
	Supreme Court declares Title I of NIRA unconstitutional
1936	Supreme Court declares AAA unconstitutional
	FDR elected for second term
1937	Court reform announced in February and rejected by the Senate in July
	FDR makes Chicago speech
	Formation of National Committee to Uphold Constitutional Government
1939	Outbreak of war in Europe
	Creation of the Executive Office of the presidency
1940	Destroyer Deal, trading 50 ships for British colonial territory
	FDR elected for third term
1941	Lend-Lease Act
	Atlantic Charter agreed
1943	FDR, Churchill and Stalin meet at Teheran to map out strategy
1944	FDR elected for fourth term
1945	Meeting at Yalta by 'Big Three' to discuss post-war world

WHEN Franklin Roosevelt took office, the job of president was smaller than when he left. The Federal Government, as a whole, was much smaller, and the role of the president in

Arthur M. Schlesinger Jr., *The Imperial Presidency* (Houghton-Mifflin, 1973)

In this book, Schlesinger — a liberal historian and friend of President Kennedy — looks at the history of the office of president and what it means to America. He argues that there has been a growth in the size and centralisation of the Federal Government, and in the power of the office of president, to such an extent that presidents have become increasingly isolated and unaccountable. Although Schlesinger looks especially at the Cold War, he argues that growth in power comes from times of national emergency when Congress and the public allow the president to expand his power to deal with it.

This book made the phrase 'imperial presidency' popular. By looking at how the power of the Executive has grown at the expense of the Legislature, Schlesinger analyses a massively important development in American history and politics. This book has become a standard text on the power of the president.

making legislation was much more limited. Many would agree that FDR created an 'imperial presidency' by creating a large federal bureaucracy that he presided over. Under his administration, the Federal Government took an active and leading role in the economy and in the welfare of the people. FDR also brought foreign policy to the forefront and made the United States a leader in world affairs. Patrick J. Maney, in *The Roosevelt Presence: The Life and Legacy of FDR* (1992), quotes diplomat George Kennan who said:

'When times were hard, as they often were, groans and lamentations went up to God, but never to Washington.'

FDR changed that. After FDR, people expected the Federal Government to help them, and they looked to the president in particular.

The American Government has a system of 'checks and balances' and 'separation of powers', which means no branch of the government – Administration, Legislature or Judiciary – should overwhelmingly dominate. However, the balance altered at times and, before FDR, the role of the president within the United States and within the constitution had been expanding. Both Theodore Roosevelt and Woodrow Wilson had developed the office, particularly in regard to foreign policy. According to Patrick J. Maney, FDR revitalised the office and made it equal to the other branches of government.

Arthur M. Schlesinger Jr., in *The Imperial Presidency* (1973), believes that the growth of presidential power comes about in response to a crisis (see **Landmark Study** above). With the Depression and World War II, FDR faced two of the three greatest crises the United States had ever faced (the third being the Civil War). It is hardly surprising that, given the challenges that FDR faced, Congress and the people were willing and even eager for him to take charge.

Ronald Edsforth, in *The New Deal: America's Response to the Great Depression* (2000), says that during FDR's first inauguration speech, the part that got the loudest cheer was when he asked for 'broad Executive power' to deal with the emergency. In fact, on 8 February 1933, before the inauguration in March, the 'lame duck' Senate passed a resolution asking FDR to take unlimited power. With the economy in crisis and 14 million people unemployed, the American people wanted someone to tell them what to do.

In modern wars, the need to allocate men and materials to the fight, security concerns and military strategy, all contrive to expand the function and size of the Federal Government. Add to this the fact that FDR was the kind of man who liked to be involved, who liked to control his associates and their decisions, and who believed that the US had an important role to play in world affairs, and it can be seen that the growth of the presidential office in the 1930s was as much a product of foreign as domestic policy.

In *The New Deal* (1998), Fiona Venn says that the extension of federal and presidential power was a response to an emergency and not planned, but it created the modern presidency. As William E. Leuchtenburg, in *Franklin D. Roosevelt and the New Deal, 1932–1940* (1963), says:

> [FDR] recreated the modern presidency. He took an office which had lost much of its prestige and power in the previous 12 years and gave it an importance which went well beyond what even Theodore Roosevelt and Woodrow Wilson had done.

How did FDR expand presidential power in domestic politics?

How did FDR's new legislation change the balance of power?

FDR was elected in 1932 to give a 'New Deal' to the American people. Mass unemployment, farm foreclosures, bankruptcies, collapse of the stock market and international trade, were just a few of the problems that the new Democratic administration faced. To deal with these issues FDR would need Congress to pass a mass of social and economic legislation. Some of the ideas originated in Congress but much came from the White House. According to Ronald Edsforth, in *The New Deal: America's Response to the Great Depression* (2000):

This bundle of legislation transformed the role of Federal Government in American life, and the balance of power within the Federal Government itself.

Federal Reserve System: a US banking system that has various banking responsibilities, including supervising US monetary policy and supervising banks that are members of the System.

Gold standard: the use of gold as the standard value for the money of a country, i.e. the dollar is worth a set amount of gold.

Raft: programme or batch of legislation.

The Emergency Banking Act extended presidential power over banks, particularly with the establishment of the **Federal Reserve System** (although Patrick J. Maney, in *The Roosevelt Presence: The Life and Legacy of FDR* (1992), says that the Emergency Banking Act came from the Senate and not from the Administration). The President also took control of monetary policy and took America off the **gold standard** by issuing an Executive Order, rather than a Congressional Act. There was opposition to the President taking such control over the banking system but the Supreme Court upheld FDR's policies and, according to William E. Leuchtenburg, in *Franklin D. Roosevelt and the New Deal, 1932–1940* (1963), the financial centre of the United States shifted from Wall Street to Washington.

FDR did far more than just deal with the banks. The **raft** of New Deal laws and agencies gave him power to provide relief (e.g. jobs, food, and shelter), adjust agricultural prices, and revive industry. Through the Tennessee Valley Authority (TVA) and the Rural Electrification Administration (REA), the Federal Government went into the business of providing power. The Works Progress Administration (WPA) gave the Federal Government a role in the arts. The National Industrial Recovery Act and the National Labor Relations Act saw the Federal Government regulating relations between employers and trade unions. And, for the first time in American history, the Federal Government involved itself directly in the provision of welfare with the Social Security Act of 1935. This was an Act FDR himself was heavily involved in creating. It is clear that in dealing with the Depression, FDR increased enormously the size of the Federal Government. The legislation also changed the relationship between the White House and Congress. Both Michael J. Heale, in *Franklin D. Roosevelt: The New Deal and War* (1999), and William E. Leuchtenburg, in *Franklin D. Roosevelt and the New Deal, 1932–1940* (1963), agree that, from the 1930s on, presidents were expected to give a detailed legislative programme to Congress. FDR had extended the president's legislative function, and the White House became the focus of government.

The relationship between the Federal Government and the states also changed under FDR. Fiona Venn, in *The New Deal* (1998), points out that the cooperation of the states was essential in implementing FDR's policies. The Federal Government was not big

The American Government: a brief introduction

- The United States is a federal state. This means political power is split between a central, or federal, government and 50 state governments. State governments have direct responsibility for social security, education and law and order within their own state. During the 20th century, the Federal Government became involved in these areas of policy.

- The USA chooses a president every four years. The president is elected in early November and takes up office on 20 January. In 1933, FDR was the last president to take up office in March. The twentieth amendment to the US constitution, passed in 1933, changed inaugural day to 20 January.

- The president chooses the government. The leading members of the government form the Cabinet. The president also has many personal advisers. These usually work for the Executive Office of the president.

- Unlike Britain, no government member can be a member of the national parliament called Congress. This idea is called the 'separation of powers'. In practice, it means the president can govern only with the cooperation of Congress.

- Congress comprises the Senate (100 members) and the House of Representatives (435 members).

- The House of Representatives and one third of the Senate are elected every two years. Each state elects two senators. The House comprises of 435 Congressmen, who are chosen on a basis of state population. Populous states, such as California and New York, have many more congressmen than states such as Montana or Rhode Island.

- The president can propose legislation but Congress passes these proposals into law.

- A president can veto Congressional legislation but, if two thirds of Congress agrees, the presidential veto can be overridden.

- Even if the president and Congress agree, the US Supreme Court can declare a law or action by the president as unconstitutional.

enough to do the job alone, so it was dependent on the states to carry out policies such as the Federal Emergency Relief Act of 1933. Federal officials and workers from the dozens of New Deal agencies, such as the Agricultural Adjustment Administration, travelled around the country to work with and help the state governments enforce federal policy. Therefore, not only did the size of the Federal Government increase and the range of its functions expand under FDR, but it also increased its influence over the states.

To what extent was the expansion criticised?

This expansion was not without criticism. By 1935, the Republicans were accusing FDR of making the Federal Government too big, and the Liberty League was formed to fight this tendency. The League was, according to Michael Simpson in *Franklin D. Roosevelt* (1989), mainly comprised of rich Easterners who opposed FDR's labour and tax policies. Criticism also came from the left. Some likened the expansion to the brand of state fascism operated by Mussolini in Italy. Nothing united FDR's critics more than his fight with the Supreme Court.

The nine judges of the Supreme Court earned FDR's wrath by rejecting much of the New Deal legislation that he saw as crucial to American recovery. Between 1935 and 1936, the Federal Government lost eight of 10 cases before the Court. These cases included the Agricultural Adjustment Act 1933, which the judges declared unconstitutional by six votes to three, and the National Industrial Recovery Act, 9–0. The Tennessee Valley Authority only just survived by five votes to four, and FDR was convinced that the Social Security and National Labor Relations Acts were about to be struck down. So, in 1937, FDR proposed to reform the Court by giving himself the power to appoint a new judge to any federal court where an existing judge was aged over 70 and refused to retire. He also wished to appoint six new Supreme Court justices, bringing the total to 15 and giving him a Court that would not prove so obstructive.

It was argued then, and since, that FDR was after revenge because the Court was not doing what he wanted. The Senate Judiciary Committee seemed to agree. In a scathing report, they called FDR's plan:

> ... a needless, futile and utterly dangerous abandonment of constitutional principle ... without precedent or justification.

In fact, the plan was not without precedent. Ronald Edsforth, in *The New Deal: America's Response to the Great Depression*

William Howard Taft (1857–1930)		
Taft trained as a lawyer, and became a Federal Circuit judge at 34 years old. In 1900, President McKinley sent him to the Philippines as Chief Civil Administrator and, from	1904 to 1908, he held the post of Secretary of War for Theodore Roosevelt. He became the twenty-seventh president in 1909, and held office until 1913 when, although he was renominated by his Party, he lost to Democrat	Woodrow Wilson. He then became a professor of Law at Yale University until President Harding made him Chief Justice of the United States. He held the position until just before his death in 1930.

(2000), shows that both President **William Howard Taft** and President Theodore Roosevelt had wanted compulsory retirement for the Supreme Court. Also, in 1924, Senator Robert La Follette had introduced measures to allow a two-thirds Congressional majority to overturn Supreme Court decisions. There had been 100 court reform Bills up till 1936, and the composition of the Court had been changed six times. This is not, however, to diminish FDR's **antipathy** to the conservative Court. As early as 1934, FDR had said he would ignore the Supreme Court if it overturned his abandoning of the gold standard.

Antipathy: hostility, opposition.

Congressmen and politicians were not only angry at the proposals but also at the way FDR introduced his reforms. He had clearly made

THAT COMPASS DOESN'T POINT THE WAY I WANT TO GO. CHANGE IT. NOW!

© 1999 J.N. "Ding" Darling Foundation

Cartoon of FDR's 1937 'Court packing plan' and opposition to it. FDR, as president, was steering the ship of the country, but its compass (the Supreme Court) was preventing him from steering it in the direction he wanted. He therefore proposed to reform the Court to his advantage.

up his mind in 1936, but waited until after the election. Anthony J. Badger, in *The New Deal: The Depression Years, 1933–1940* (1989), says that the massive election victory made FDR believe he had public support for his measures, but he did not. FDR surprised Congress when he introduced his Court Reform Bill in February 1937. The reaction was immediate and angry. Ronald Edsforth, in *The New Deal: America's Response to the Great Depression* (2000), says that there was anger at the lack of consultation and at the expectation by FDR that Congress would simply go along with his wishes. William E. Leuchtenberg, in *Franklin D. Roosevelt and the New Deal 1932–1940* (1963), also says there was anger at FDR's dishonesty in presenting the Bill as an efficiency issue, which it clearly was not. Even FDR's own supporters in Congress, such as Democratic Congressman Samuel Pettergill from Indiana, denounced the 'Court packing plan' as an attack on the constitution. The fight went on for 24 weeks, with FDR using all his charm, promises of patronage and even threats to get it his way. But Congress refused to give in and, in July, FDR backed down.

In this case, FDR appears to have failed to extend his presidential power. However, there is much debate about the outcome of the fight. In spite of the administration's fears, the Social Security Act and the National Labor Relations Act were not struck down by the Court. Also, in May 1937, the conservative judge Justice Willis Van Devanter announced retirement. As more elderly judges retired over the following three years, FDR was able to appoint his own men. He appointed five justices of the Supreme Court and, according to Ronald Edsforth and Anthony J. Badger, made the Court in later years more liberal. However, William E. Leuchtenburg, in *Franklin D. Roosevelt and the New Deal, 1932–1940* (1963), says that FDR did not win because, although the judges passed cases, Congress was angry and passed fewer of FDR's laws for the Court to consider.

FDR had badly damaged his political reputation and was subject to charges of acting like a dictator. Michael Simpson, in *Franklin D. Roosevelt* (1989), says that FDR's immense political skills had deserted him in this fight. What he should have done was let the Supreme Court overturn more legislation, especially the Social Security Act and the National Labor Relations Act, to allow the public and Congress to see that the New Deal was being destroyed. This would have increased support for the President and his reform proposals. Others argue that he could simply have waited for the old, conservative judges to retire. In the Internet article 'Roosevelt's Expansion of the Presidency' (2003), Russell D. Renka argues that FDR did hope to change public opinion about the Court in the long term, but in the short term he wanted to scare the judges into backing off from damaging the New Deal. More importantly, he was not planning to stand for a third term, so taking on the Court in 1937 was essential if he were to effect real change. Renka also maintains that even though the fight did damage FDR politically, we should not overestimate this. His loss of popularity in 1937/8 was more to do with the recession and his stand on race than his fight with the Supreme Court.

Anger at FDR's 'Court packing plan' pushed Southern Democrats and Republicans closer together. The two groups began to work together in Congress, forming what became known as the 'conservative coalition'. Their combined votes blocked many New Deal policies and were a major reason why the New Deal slowed down so dramatically after 1937. This period is sometimes known as the 'Third New Deal'. There were some important measures, such as the Fair Labor Standards Act, but nothing on the scale of the First or Second New Deals was established. For his part, FDR was angry at the rejection of his Court Reform Bill and at the way the Southern Democrats were working with Republicans to weaken New Deal measures, especially on race and labour. The Fair Labor Standards Act, for example, was limited to exclude domestic and agricultural workers. In a 'fireside chat' in July 1938, FDR talked of the need to 'purge' conservatives from the Party and to make it more liberal. According to William E. Leuchtenburg, in *Franklin D. Roosevelt and the New Deal, 1932–1940*, (1963), FDR was trying to create a national, centralised Party – an idea that had started with Harry Hopkins. Again, FDR's policy and conduct convinced opponents that he was assuming dictatorial powers. (As William Leuchtenburg points out, the use of the word 'purge' had particularly unfortunate connotations with Hitler in power.)

FDR targeted five Southern senators and one congressman, who he thought he could defeat, and he travelled to campaign against their nomination for the 1938 mid-terms. In *Franklin D. Roosevelt* (1989), Michael Simpson says that FDR should not have gone in person but should have had the local Party organisation do the job. It is very doubtful if this would have had any effect. As Fiona Venn shows, in *The New Deal* (1998), this interference in Congressional elections was against tradition. FDR had clearly gone beyond the powers of his office. The candidates that he had hoped to purge were, with one exception, elected by their constituents. Relations with Congress grew even more antagonistic. From 1938, very little legislation, from the President to **the Hill**, was passed.

The Hill: Capitol Hill is where the Capitol building, which houses Congress, is situated.

How was the Executive Branch reformed?

While FDR was fighting with Congress over the Supreme Court and over the mid-terms, he also introduced a measure to reform the Executive Branch of the US Government, which was his own area of responsibility. According to Patrick J. Maney, in *The Roosevelt Presence: The Life and Legacy of FDR* (1992), FDR liked order, and the Executive Branch needed modernising due to the haphazard nature of the New Deal. (The New Deal had been set up without always having clear lines of responsibility or authority.) The reorganisation would have given FDR more staff in the White House and brought all the New Deal agencies under White House control. A committee had been set up to make recommendations, and its proposals would have increased presidential control of the budget and of federal personnel and administration. It would also have increased the Federal Government's role in the economy and its control of natural resources. According to Richard D. Polenberg, in *The Era of Franklin D. Roosevelt* (2000), FDR also saw better organisation as a way of achieving more social reform. Most historians agree with Anthony J. Badger, in *The New Deal: The Depression Years, 1933–1940* (1989), that the proposals were 'modest and reasonable', but as Patrick J. Maney, in *The Roosevelt Presence: The Life and Legacy of FDR* (1992), says:

> Coinciding as they did with his campaign for Court reform at home, and the rise of totalitarianism abroad, Executive reorganisation struck some critics as a step towards dictatorship.

The National Committee to Uphold Constitutional Government was set up in 1937 to fight the proposals, and the proposals were defeated. The vote, 204–196 including 108 Democrats, was one of biggest Party defections in history and indicated the fear and hostility FDR now aroused. Instead, in 1939, FDR used his own power to issue Executive Order 8248, setting up the Executive Office of the president. In *Franklin D. Roosevelt and the New Deal, 1932–1940* (1963), William E. Leuchtenburg calls the establishment of the Executive Office 'epoch making'. It gave the President six staff assistants, and brought under White House control the Bureau of the Budget and the National Resources Planning Board. Although the latter was later removed, the Order allowed future presidents to bring other federal organisations under their authority, such as the Central Intelligence Agency (CIA), the National Security Council (NSC) and the National Education Association (NEA). The Executive Office, which is housed in the West Wing of the White House, has now become an indispensable part of the Federal Government, and whatever FDR's critics argued, it was, as Russell D. Renka, in 'Roosevelt's Expansion of the Presidency' (2003), states:

> ... a necessary organisational modernising of an office which bore vastly expanded administrative responsibilities in 1939 compared to 1932.

How did FDR expand presidential power in foreign affairs?

How did presidential power expand in response to World War II?

According to Patrick J. Maney, in *The Roosevelt Presence: The Life and Legacy of FDR* (1992):

> [FDR] made one thing clear from the outset; in his administration, foreign policy would emanate from the White House.

Initially, FDR's foreign policy had some important successes. Introduced in 1933, the Good Neighbour Policy in Latin America made relations on the continent the best they had been for some time. Also, in 1933, the US formally recognised the Soviet Union. However, Robert Dallek, in *Franklin D. Roosevelt and American Foreign Policy, 1932–1945* (1995), says that FDR had no interest at all in Cuba even though a new American-backed government was set up there in 1934, and FDR only recognised the USSR after wide consultation to gauge public opinion. With regard to the Good Neighbour Policy, many believe that FDR was simply continuing Herbert Hoover's policy of improved relations. However, FDR took a much greater interest in events in Europe and the Far East as he believed they presented the greatest threat to US security.

Although FDR would like to have pursued a more activist policy towards Europe, his hands had been tied by the Neutrality Acts. The support for the Ludlow amendment, and the outcry that greeted his 1937 speech in Chicago, showed FDR how carefully he had to tread. According to James T. Patterson, in *America in the Twentieth Century* (1994), isolationists worried that war would extend presidential power further than FDR's domestic policy had already done. Their fears seemed realised when FDR misled them by saying he would not get the US involved in the war but then introduced secret military talks with the British and French. In

April 1941, there was an Executive Agreement for US bases to be established in Greenland. In July, American troops were stationed in Iceland and, in the autumn, it was revealed that US ships had been escorting British convoys. Given the support for the Neutrality Acts and the Ludlow amendment, and the reaction to his Chicago speech, FDR had little choice but to be less than open about his policies. James T. Patterson, in *America in the Twentieth Century* (1994), says that given the opposition from isolationists, and considering the kind of man Hitler was, FDR had little choice but to use his power the way he did. However, he also admits that by letting the end justify the means FDR:

> ... set precedents for presidential aggrandisement and dishonesty, which later occupants of the White House were to emulate for ignobler ends.

When the war actually did come, Michael Simpson, in *Franklin D. Roosevelt* (1989), asserts that FDR took much more interest in the day-to-day running of war than any other president had done in the past. When British military visitors, who had come to discuss strategy, complained, in 1942, of the disorganisation in American military leadership, FDR streamlined the command structure and set up the Joint Chiefs of Staff. He did this personally without Congress or Executive Order, although, as Commander in Chief of the military, the President was free to make many operational decisions. FDR appointed some very talented men, such as General George Marshall and Admiral Chester Nimitz, but he would sometimes take tactical decisions against their advice.

In 1942/3, FDR was under great pressure from Stalin to open a 'second front' to take pressure off the Red Army. According to Patrick J. Maney, in *The Roosevelt Presence: The Life and Legacy of FDR* (1992), General Marshall also wanted to invade Europe in 1943. Churchill, however, did not believe the Allies were ready and suggested an invasion of North Africa to improve morale, give the American military more experience and enable the Allies to launch an attack in Southern Europe. Patrick Maney and Michael Heale both agree that FDR went against the advice of his generals in supporting Churchill. However, once the decisions had been taken, FDR did not interfere in the day-to-day running of military tactics and let his generals get on with the fight.

When FDR discussed America's post-war role he was initially unclear. He believed cooperation with the USSR was vital as he felt the USSR would replace Britain as the other major power. When FDR, Churchill and Stalin met at Teheran in 1943, James T.

Churchill, FDR and Stalin at Yalta, 1945. At this crucial meeting their discussions laid the foundations for the post-war world.

Patterson, in *America in the Twentieth Century* (1994), says that FDR was deliberately vague about American intentions, except to say that he did not believe the American public would want troops in Europe beyond 1947. Also, although the Atlantic Charter talked about an international organisation as early as 1941, Robert Dallek and James Patterson agree that FDR's support was cautious to say the least. Patrick J. Maney, in *The Roosevelt Presence: The Life and Legacy of FDR* (1992), says that when FDR talked about the creation of the United Nations, he was careful not to raise expectations and make the same mistake as Wilson had done with the League of Nations in 1919. But, even with this caution, Maney does not believe FDR would have been able to get the Senate to ratify the UN Charter due to their hostility to the President. America's participation in the organisation owes more to Truman than to FDR.

With the agreement reached at Yalta in 1945 many argue that, far from expanding American power, FDR in fact gave far too much to Stalin. FDR was naïve in his dealings with the Soviet leader, thinking he would be able to charm him. He has been criticised for giving too much to Stalin, including a secret deal, which the Chinese were not told about, where the USSR would get southern Sakhalin and the Kurile Islands and have supremacy in Manchuria. Critics also feel that the agreement left open to too much interpretation the question of German reparations. Above all, FDR is accused of betraying Eastern Europe, in particular Poland, where he only managed to get vague promises of free elections that Stalin later went back on. However, James Patterson, Patrick Maney, and others, all agree on the limits of presidential power in this case. The reality was that Stalin's troops controlled Poland and most of Eastern Europe. FDR was not allowing Stalin anything he did not already have. Maney says that FDR saw the future as fluid and hoped that once the Soviets felt more secure they would be more amenable to change in Eastern Europe. Instead, FDR created unrealistic expectations of the post-war settlement. He should have made the public more aware of the limitations of American power.

How did FDR expand presidential power on the home front in response to World War II?

The greatest leap in presidential power was in fact seen on the home front rather than on the battlefield or in the conference room. Michael J. Heale, in *Franklin D. Roosevelt: The New Deal and War* (1999), and Patrick J. Maney, in *The Roosevelt Presence: The Life and Legacy of FDR* (1992), show the range of operations that came under the power of the White House during World War II. FDR set up the War Production Board, the Office of Economic Stabilisation, the Office of War Mobilisation and the Office of Price Administration. He also expanded the Reconstruction Finance Corporation. Congress granted him the power to control conscription, raw materials, manpower, prices, rents and the rationing of consumer goods. According to Patrick J. Maney, in *The Roosevelt Presence: The Life and Legacy of FDR* (1992), giving the President these powers meant that debates only went on inside the White House. As with the New Deal, FDR established large and competing agencies that reported directly to him so that ultimate control was in his hands. However, this does not mean that FDR got exactly what he wanted. His proposal for a national service law, which would have allowed him to direct all workers, was refused by Congress. His proposal for an Economic Bill of Rights, which would have extended the right to education, jobs and welfare to all American citizens, was also refused. (FDR saw economic security as a method of reducing conflict and as a reward to those who fought.) Congress also passed a tax Bill over the presidential veto in 1944.

In spite of these setbacks, presidential and federal power grew dramatically. Even though many domestic proposals failed, non-defence spending still rose from $7.2 to $17 billion. The Bureau of the Budget was reorganised and reported to the President instead of the Treasury. According to Russell D. Renka, in 'Roosevelt's Expansion of the Presidency' (2003), the administration was responding to the needs of the war. James T. Patterson, in *America in the Twentieth Century* (1994), says that the growth in federal power was allowed to happen because only the White House seemed able to carry on the war externally and internally. According to Michael Simpson, in *Franklin D. Roosevelt* (1989), FDR was crucial in mobilising war effort. However, Simpson states:

> The White House now sheltered a powerful, pervasive and permanent bureaucracy; the 'imperial presidency' was now emerging.

Assessment

FDR had entered the White House with the firm belief that the power of the Federal Government could be used for good. However, the Federal Government was small and the Executive had a limited role relative to the Legislature. To enact the New Deal, FDR had to create new structures and employ far more people. This expansion in federal power was extended by the practical needs of fighting a 'total war'. Any president facing the two challenges of the Depression and World War II would have had to stretch the powers of government to handle the crises, and there is no doubt that the role and responsibilities of the Federal Government grew dramatically under FDR. But FDR went much further than other presidents might have done. He also expanded the power of his own office relative to the other branches of government, notably Congress. In *The Roosevelt Presence: The Life and Legacy of FDR* (1992), Patrick J. Maney says that although FDR did not create the modern presidency, he revitalised it and made it equal to the other branches of government. Much of the legislation of the New Deal was initiated by the White House and, although FDR gave his advisers a lot of freedom, he kept the final decisions in his own hands. When the Supreme Court or Congress opposed him he fought back, even though he was not always successful.

Due to the international situation in 1940, FDR decided to break with tradition and stand for a third term. Although he misled his Party over his intention to do so, William E. Leuchtenburg, in *Franklin D. Roosevelt and the New Deal 1932–1940* (1963), says that no one else was up to the job, and FDR won the election with a convincing, if reduced, majority of five million votes. In spite of failing health, FDR was even elected an unprecedented fourth time, in 1944, by a people who wanted him to see out the war. However, one man holding such a powerful office for 12 years, in which he expanded its functions so radically, was sufficient for Congress and the states to want to ensure that there were some limits placed on presidential power. The twenty-second amendment, ratified in 1951, limited all future presidents to two terms.

FDR pursued an active foreign policy. He used the power of the Executive to support Churchill as far as he could, even to the extent of keeping information from the American public. He met with Stalin at Yalta and laid the foundations of the post-war world. Add to all this, his effective use of the radio and press to get support for his policies, and his four election victories; and it is clear that FDR was unlike any president who had gone before. In the 1940s, Congress would try to reassert its authority, causing many problems for President Truman. However, although Congress had several victories, FDR had changed irrevocably the role of the president.

Was FDR the first imperial president?

1. Read the following extract and answer the question.

'I am far from intimating that the President of the United States is incapable of selecting suitable men for the Supreme Court. I am simply accepting his own word and that of his spokesmen to the effect that he wants men "biased" on behalf of his legislative and administrative projects, who may be counted on to reverse the Supreme Court decisions already rendered and give such other decisions of policy as may be desired.'

(From a speech by Carter Glass, Democrat senator for Virginia, March 29, 1937.)

Using the information in the extract above, and from this section, explain the objections to FDR's Court Reform Bill.

2. Was FDR the first imperial president? Give reasons for your answer.

FDR: an assessment

Was the New Deal successful?

Through the '100 days', FDR used the power of the Federal Government to introduce a wide range of policies and agencies to put the unemployed back to work, to cut production in agriculture and industry, and to restore faith in the banking system. In these policies, FDR had to balance the needs of various groups, such as town dwellers versus farmers, employers versus unions, national versus local needs, etc. His policies were not always successful because of this.

FDR's success was also limited by his conflicts with the Supreme Court and his own Party. By attempting to 'pack' the Court, and then by trying to manipulate the Democratic Party into choosing only his supporters, FDR left himself open to accusations of dictatorship, and support for his policies ebbed away.

Although the New Deal did not bring about economic recovery, it physically changed the United States through the building and conservation work that went on. More importantly, the New Deal introduced the view that it was the responsibility of the Federal Government to look after the poor and weak.

FDR as interventionalist?

In foreign policy, FDR believed that governments could work for good, and he believed that the United States should take an active role in the world to defend democracy and maintain peace.

In domestic and foreign affairs, FDR was always conscious of the public mood so he was not always open about the support he gave to the British before America entered World War II. Although this support was crucial to Britain, FDR left a dangerous precedent that was followed with much less honourable intent by Johnson and Nixon in Vietnam.

FDR as imperial president?

In the creation of the New Deal, and the extension of the power of his office to be able to fight the war, FDR massively increased the size, role and prestige of the Federal Government. In both domestic and foreign affairs, the American people now look to the Federal Government for answers in a way they had never done before.

FDR shifted the balance of power from state government to the Federal Government in Washington, and from Congress to the White House. He made the office of president of the United States the most powerful position in America.

Further reading

Texts specifically designed for students

Degler, C.N. *Out of Our Past* (Harper & Row, 1984)
Heale, M.J. *Franklin D. Roosevelt: The New Deal and War*
(Routledge, 1999)
Patterson, J.T. *America in the Twentieth Century* (Harcourt Brace,
1994)
Simpson, M. *Franklin D. Roosevelt* (Blackwell, 1989)
Venn, F. *The New Deal* (Edinburgh University Press, 1998)

Texts for more advanced study

Badger, A.J. *The New Deal: The Depression Years, 1933–1940*
(Macmillan, 1989) looks at New Deal policies thematically, and
emphasises the compromises that FDR had to make.
Dallek, R. *Franklin D. Roosevelt and American Foreign Policy,
1932–1945* (Oxford University Press, 1995 (second edition)) is an
admiring and detailed study of FDR's foreign policy.
Edsforth, R. *The New Deal: America's Response to the Great
Depression* (Blackwell, 2000) details the New Deal, and has an
excellent first section on the Depression that shows the scale of
the crisis facing FDR and therefore the scale of his achievement.
Leuchtenburg, W.E. *Franklin D. Roosevelt and the New Deal,
1932–1940* (Harper & Row, 1963) is a chronologically study that
is critical of the New Deal's weaknesses, but also emphasises the
New Deal's successes and how it laid foundations for the future.
Maney, P.J. *The Roosevelt Presence: The Life and Legacy of FDR*
(University of California Press, 1992) is a biography of FDR with a
very useful timeline and extensive bibliography.
Parrish, M.E. *Anxious Decades: America in Prosperity and
Depression, 1920–1941* (W.W. Norton & Company, 1992) is a
general text on US history with detailed sections on FDR.
Polenberg, R.D. *The Era of Franklin D. Roosevelt, 1933–1945: A
Brief History With Documents* (Bedford St Martins, 2000)
contains a range of documents with a section on FDR's policies.
Russell D. Renka 'Roosevelt's Expansion of the Presidency'
(Southeast Missouri State University, 2003) is a paper for
students taking a course in 'The Modern Presidency'.

Index